DATE DUE

SEP 1 0 2010	
JUL 2 0 2011	

The Last Lieutenant

The Last Lieutenant

*A Foxhole View of the
Epic Battle for
Iwo Jima*

John C. Shively

Indiana University Press
BLOOMINGTON AND INDIANAPOLIS

This book is a publication of

Indiana University Press
601 North Morton Street
Bloomington, IN 47404-3797 USA

http://iupress.indiana.edu

Telephone orders   800-842-6796
Fax orders   812-855-7931
Orders by e-mail   iuporder@indiana.edu

The paper used in this publication meets the minimum
requirements of American National Standard for Information Sciences—Permanence of Paper for Printed Library
Materials, ANSI Z39.48-1984.

Manufactured in the United States of America

Library of Congress Cataloging-in-Publication Data

Shively, John C., date
  The last lieutenant : a foxhole view of the epic battle for
Iwo Jima / John C. Shively.
       p. cm.
  Includes bibliographical references.
  ISBN 0-253-34728-9 (cloth : alk. paper) 1. Craig, James
R. (James Richard), 1923– 2. World War, 1939–1945—
Campaigns—Japan. 3. Iwo Jima, Battle of, Japan, 1945.
4. United States. Marine Corps. Division, 4th.
5. Marines—United States—Biography. I. Title.
  D767.2.S55 2006
  940.54'2528—dc22   2005026652

1 2 3 4 5 11 10 09 08 07 06

This book is for
Jim and Pat Craig's children,
Tim, Pete, Katy, Annie, Sally, and Tom.

This book is respectfully dedicated to the memory of those
Marines of the 1st Platoon, L Company, 3rd Battalion,
24th Regiment, 4th Marine Division.
Semper Fidelis

The Final Inspection

The Marine stood and faced his God,
Which must always come to pass,
He hoped his shoes were shining bright
just as brightly as his brass.

"Step forward now, Marine,
how shall I deal with you?
Have you turned the other cheek?
To my church have you been true?"

The Marine squared his shoulders and said,
"No, Lord, I guess I ain't
because those of us who carry guns
can't always be a saint.

"I've had to work most Sundays
And at times my talk was rough,
I've had to break your rules, my Lord,
because the world is awfully tough.

"I never passed a cry for help,
though at times I shook with fear,
and sometimes, God forgive me,
I've wept unmanly tears.

"I know I don't deserve a place
among the people here;
they never wanted me around
except to calm their fears.

"If you've a place for me, Lord,
It needn't be so grand,
I never expected or had too much,
But if you don't, I'll understand."

There was a silence all around the throne
Where the saints often trod
As the Marine waited quietly,
For the judgment of his God.

"Step forward now, Marine,"
God proclaimed.
"You've borne your burdens well.
Come walk peacefully on Heaven's streets.
You've done your time in HELL."

Author Unknown

Contents

Acknowledgments

This book could not have been written without the help of many people who at one time or another provided encouragement, research assistance, and editorial advice. I am grateful to my uncle, James R. Craig, who agreed to tell me his story so that I could write it. He put up with my awkward first attempt at interviewing as I stumbled through the early stages of our discussions about his involvement in the war generally and the battle of Iwo Jima specifically. My special thanks to Jim's wife, Pat, who graciously tolerated my intrusions into their home on Saturday mornings and provided delicious lunches.

The staff of the Marine Corps University archives department at Quantico, Virginia, provided invaluable assistance on two occasions. Pat Mullen helped me, via e-mail, with my first experience in an archive. Belinda Kelly photocopied oversized maps and other documents for me. Mike Miller was very helpful when I returned to scan official combat photographs.

The staff at the National Archives on the campus of the University of Maryland in College Park provided archival material, including death records of the Marines of the 4th Division killed on Iwo Jima.

Ruth Dixson of Bloomington, Indiana, provided photographs of Iwo Jima taken by her late husband when he was on Iwo Jima in 1945 with the U.S. Army.

I am indebted to two great Marines for their contribution: Lt. Col. Brian Joseph, a good friend since our high school days together, and Col. Scott Reske, a fellow triathlete and a friend of Jim's family from Pendleton, Indiana. Both critiqued the manuscript and corrected its many errors, both military and otherwise. They made sure I got the Marine stuff right.

A good friend, Jack Kerins of Terre Haute, Indiana, and a 3rd Marine Division veteran of four Pacific campaigns including Guadalcanal and Bougainville in the Solomon Islands, Guam, and Iwo Jima, read the manuscript and provided editorial advice and encouragement.

Captain Thomas Fisher of the United States Marine Corps, Purdue Navy ROTC, provided me with information about platoon leader responsibilities.

Two people whose opinions I value read the manuscript and offered encouragement. My roommate in the Marianas, Virgil Anderson, a World War II Marine veteran, and Bob Sanders, who flew missions over Germany as a World War II B-17 bomber pilot, both read an early version and provided much appreciated encouragement.

As they have for all of the manuscripts that I have written, my parents, John and Virginia Shively, read this one and pointed out my many spelling and grammatical errors. My sister-in-law, Misty Shively, pointed out more errors.

A special thanks to my editor at Indiana University Press, Bob Sloan, and his assistant, Jane Quinet, who were very patient as they guided me through the publication process.

Lastly, I would like to thank all the Marines I met along the way—those at Quantico, those on maneuvers on the island of Tinian in the Northern Marianas, those from Okinawa I met on Iwo Jima, the Iwo Jima veterans I met during my trip to the Marianas and Iwo Jima, and all the ex-Marines and those in the Marine Corps Reserve I have met in my office practice over the years. You guys are the greatest. I sleep more soundly and know that America is safe with you at the ready to answer the call. Semper Fi.

Note on Abbreviations

In describing individual Marine units I occasionally use standard Marine designations used by the Corps in World War II. *BLT 3/24* is the unit designation for the 3rd Battalion Landing Team of the 24th Marines, to distinguish it from the 3rd Rifle Battalion of the 24th Marines, "3/24." A battalion landing team was composed of the three rifle companies of a battalion in addition to associated supporting units.

Other times I make a reference to *RCT 24*, Regimental Combat Team 24. RCT 24 consisted of the three rifle battalions of the 24th Regiment of the 4th Division plus associated attached units including a tank battalion, engineers, a medical corps, a war dog platoon, artillery, a scout and sniper platoon, a replacement draft, and other ancillary units needed to reinforce the regiment.

D-Day is the military term for the unnamed day on which an operation or a military offensive is to be launched. Subsequent days are referred to as "D plus an integer." Days leading up to the D-Day are designated "D minus an integer." Using the same schema, *H-Hour* is the hour the battle or operation is to commence and time before and after H-Hour is H plus or minus time in minutes or hours. For example, two days before D-Day is designated as D-2 and two days after D-Day is D+2. One hour before landing is designated H-1.

The military refers to time using a 24-hour clock to avoid possible confusion. Midnight is 2400 and is pronounced "twenty-four hundred hours" and 1:45 AM is designated 0145. Noon is 1200, and 3:30 PM is designated 1530.

The Last Lieutenant

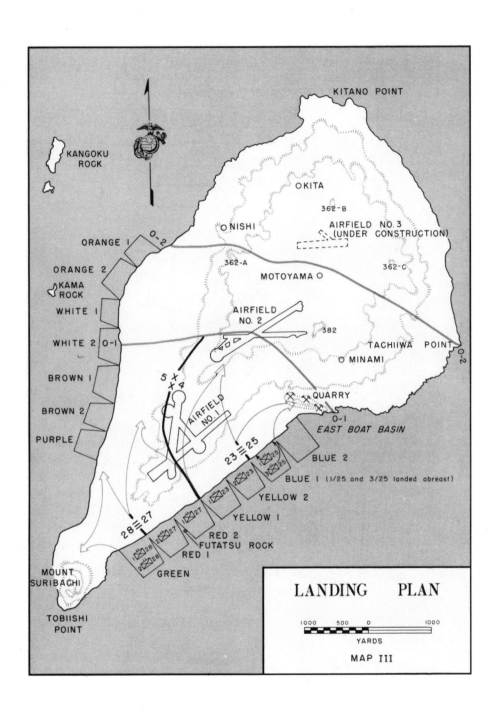

KITANO POINT

KANGOKU ROCK

OKITA

362-B

ONISHI

AIRFIELD NO.3
(UNDER CONSTRUCTION)

ORANGE 1

O-2

362-A

ORANGE 2

MOTOYAMA O

362-C

KAMA ROCK

WHITE 1

AIRFIELD NO. 2

382

WHITE 2   O-1

TACHIIWA   POINT

O-2

O MINAMI

BROWN 1

5 ✕
✕ 4

QUARRY

BROWN 2

O-1
EAST BOAT BASIN

AIRFIELD NO.1

PURPLE

23 ≡ 25

BLUE 2

3/25

1/25   3/25

BLUE 1 (1/25 and 3/25 landed abreast)

1/23   2/23

YELLOW 2

2/23

YELLOW 1

28 ≡ 27

1/27

2/27

RED 2
FUTATSU ROCK

1/28   2/28

RED 1

MOUNT SURIBACHI

3/28

GREEN

TOBIISHI POINT

LANDING   PLAN

1000   500   0   1000

YARDS

MAP III

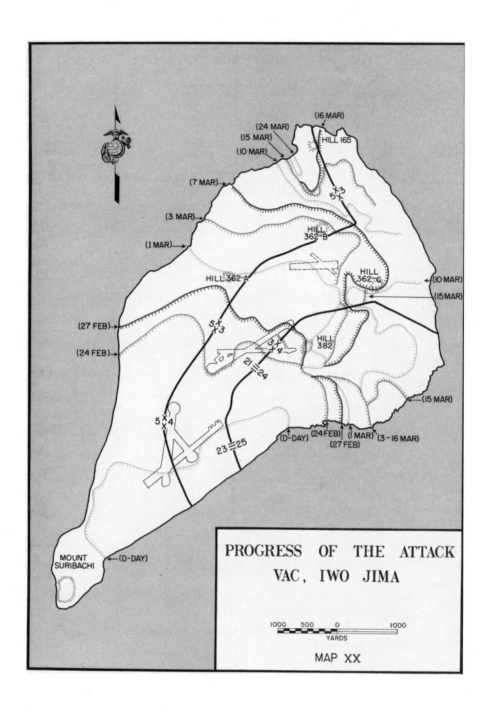

(16 MAR)

(24 MAR)
(15 MAR)
(10 MAR)
HILL 165

(7 MAR)

5 × 3

(3 MAR)

(1 MAR)
HILL 362-B

HILL 362-A
HILL 362-C
(10 MAR)
(15 MAR)

(27 FEB)
5 × 3
HILL 382

(24 FEB)
3 × 8

21 ≡ 24

5 × 4
(15 MAR)

23 ≡ 25
(D-DAY) (24 FEB) (1 MAR) (3 - 16 MAR)
(27 FEB)

MOUNT
SURIBACHI (D-DAY)

PROGRESS OF THE ATTACK
VAC, IWO JIMA

1000   500   0   1000
YARDS

MAP XX

Prologue

For as long as I can remember, I have associated the battle of Iwo Jima with my uncle Jim Craig, who served in the United States Marine Corps. It was common knowledge in our extended family that he never spoke about his experience on Iwo Jima; it apparently was an untouchable topic. I often wondered what that experience had been, but since he never seemed to talk about it, I assumed that the subject was, as it was for many veterans, too painful to discuss. So I kept my curiosity to myself.

In February 1995, on the fiftieth anniversary of the invasion of Iwo Jima, I wrote a letter to Jim thanking him for serving his country and for the sacrifice he made on her behalf. I also sent him a little framed commemorative U.S. postage stamp of Joe Rosenthal's picture of the raising of the flag over Mount Suribachi. I was pleased to get a reply from Jim a few weeks later. In it he described what it was like for him on Iwo Jima. He wrote that he survived because he ran fast, zigzagged a lot, and kept low. He added that he was proud to have served in the Marines.

My early interest in World War II was more about "the big picture" battles and the pitting of one army against another. In 2000 I read two books that changed my perspective. *The Greatest Generation* by Tom Brokaw focuses on the common citizen soldier, his experience in the war, and how it affected him. It put a human touch to the war. For the first time I began to think about the life of the individual American soldier, the unselfish sacrifices he made, and his devotion to duty and service to his country. After I read *Flags of Our Fathers*, by James Bradley, son of John Bradley, the last surviving Iwo Jima flag raiser, I decided that I wanted to write an account based on Jim's experiences.

I invited Uncle Jim and Aunt Pat to dinner in Indianapolis in July 2000 to discuss my idea with them. I arrived at the restaurant feeling nervous; I had not revealed to them what it was that I wanted to discuss. I wanted to present my idea to Jim and give him a few weeks to think about it. To my delight he immediately consented and began telling me stories about Iwo

Jima. It seemed I had released in him a long pent-up desire to tell someone about his wartime experience.

I asked him why he had been so reluctant to talk about Iwo Jima all these years. His answer surprised me, and it was embarrassingly simple. No one had ever asked him. No one had ever shown any interest in his Marine Corps experience and his involvement with the battle of Iwo Jima. He was too self-effacing to bring the subject up. He likely would have taken it to the grave and we would have been deprived of a stirring story that needed, I think, to be told. Not only is it a story about a young man going off to war on the other side of the world to fight a tenacious and resourceful enemy, but it is a story of devotion to duty, loyalty, and an uncompromising conviction.

Jim and I went to the Marine Corps base at Quantico, Virginia, where we had access to the vast resources of the archives department of the Marine Corps University. I was able to obtain copies of declassified after-action reports written in 1945. These described the daily movement of Marine units down to the company level and occasionally to the platoon level. These proved to be an invaluable source of information not found in the many commercially available books about Iwo Jima and the war in the Pacific. I also obtained copies of declassified maps of the island, which included the locations of the three airfields, villages, prominent natural features, and the suspected locations of Japanese bunkers and gun emplacements. I had access to hundreds of photographs taken by official combat photographers, including Joe Rosenthal. I scanned several of these and have included them as a supplement to the narrative because I want the reader to visualize what it was like on Iwo Jima during the battle.

Many books about Iwo Jima describe the conduct of the entire battle involving the three Marine divisions of the Fifth Amphibious Corps (VAC). From the outset I wanted this story to be narrower in scope, concerning the men of the 1st Platoon. On more than one occasion Jim reminded me that his little war was confined to an area no more than about 25 yards around his position and that he was mostly unaware of what was going on elsewhere. He had a specific job to do on a narrowly defined part of the island. I resisted the temptation to describe some of the more famous events of the battle and instead concentrated on those in which Jim and his men had participated. It is, in effect, a foxhole view of the war.

I did not intend this narrative to be an exhaustive account of the day-to-day battle record of any particular Marine outfit, but rather a series of stories as Jim remembered them. I have made every effort to place them in the general context of the ongoing battle and to match them to the chronological order in which they likely would have taken place. Consequently, this account will not read like a military textbook.

Movies and novels about World War II initially influenced my writing style. I had Jim read what I had written on an ongoing basis to make sure I was getting it right. He constantly rebuked me for making the narrative sound too "Hollywood." For Jim, combat was quite different than the way Hollywood would have us believe. Until recently, Hollywood sanitized and glorified war. The battle of Iwo Jima was anything but clean and neat. Marines did not get shot and simply fall down, as they frequently do in the movies and sometimes with dramatic flair. They often were blown to bits, horribly mutilated, and they died hideously. There was nothing about it to glory in. Accordingly, I altered some wording and removed other passages altogether to conform to the description of the battle as Jim related it to me. The only license I took was in writing the dialogue.

I have inserted dialogue to try to make the narrative more interesting and realistic without making it too "Hollywood." In some cases I used Jim's exact words as told to me during our interviews. In most cases, however, I wrote dialogue as I imagined it would have been at the time.

Of my uncles, I am closest to Jim. During the many hours spent interviewing him and reviewing the early versions of the manuscript with him, we became even closer. When a man bares his soul and describes how men under his command died and how he himself stared death squarely in the eye, one cannot avoid knowing him better. On more than one occasion we were both brought to tears by some of the stories he told.

When I started writing, I had no idea how long the narrative would be. The more I studied and the more I talked with Jim, the longer it became. He kept coming up with more stories. I was surprised not by how much he remembered after 56 years but by the level of detail that he could recall. Despite Jim's surprisingly good recollection of the many stories about Iwo Jima, there was no way he could pinpoint the exact date that certain events took place. Generally though, he could recall a particular story to within a few days of its occurrence. Clearly his best recollection of any one day was that of the events of D-Day. The recollection of events of the following week are generally clear, but the timing after that becomes a little fuzzy until the day he leaves Iwo Jima on D+27, 18 March 1945. Taking his stories and matching them with official after-action reports, I made every attempt to recount them as closely to the chronological order in which they actually took place. It is not perfect, but the precise order in which they happened is not important. What is important is that Jim recalled his experiences so vividly.

In March 2002 I visited Iwo Jima as part of a tour with Military Historical Tours for the 57th Anniversary Reunion of Honor. It was the zenith of all my work on this project. During the one-day visit I had virtually unfettered access to the island and was allowed to bring home some interesting souvenirs.

Finally, I must point out that I have no personal military experience. All that I learned about the Marine Corps and battlefield tactics came from my research and from my conversations with Jim and other Marines. It is my hope that this story will serve to honor both my uncle and the United States Marine Corps by providing a foxhole perspective of those momentous events on Iwo Jima, where, in the words of Fleet Adm. Chester W. Nimitz, "Uncommon valor was a common virtue."

1

Prelude to War

On Sunday, 7 December 1941, the USS *Arizona* with 1,177 of her crew lay in the mud on the bottom of Pearl Harbor. A few hours earlier, just before 0800, the first wave of carrier-based attack planes of the Japanese Imperial Navy had come swooping in from the north to set up their torpedo runs on Battleship Row. As the first attack wave approached the harbor, Lt. Cmdr. Mitsuo Fuchida, chief pilot on the *Akagi* and designated operational leader of the attack, broadcast the code words "Tora Tora Tora!" The repeated code word, meaning "tiger," stood for "We have succeeded in a surprise attack."[1] The second wave arrived 40 minutes later. Like the first wave, it concentrated on the moored ships in the harbor and the parked aircraft at Wheeler and Hickam airfields. The Japanese met little antiaircraft resistance and were virtually unchallenged in the air. Eighteen ships of the U.S. Pacific Fleet were either sunk or heavily damaged, including four mainline battleships now sitting on the bottom of the harbor. One hundred sixty-four Navy and Army aircraft were destroyed and 124 damaged, many while closely parked together on the tarmac. American casualties included 2,403 killed (nearly half from the *Arizona*) and 1,178 wounded.

A cogent analysis of Japanese opening tactics in its previous wars might have predicted the attack. In 1895 the Japanese fought a short war with the Chinese in which they won control of the Korean peninsula. In 1904–1905 they fought against tsarist Russia, taking over Russian spheres of influence in Manchuria and China. Both wars were preceded by a surprise attack.

On 26 November the First Air Fleet, under the command of Adm. Isoroku Yamamoto, set sail under strict radio silence from Hitokappu Bay in the Kuril Islands northeast of Japan. The fleet consisted of six aircraft carriers, accompanying escorts, and over 400 planes including torpedo bombers, high-level bombers, and dive-bombers with Zero fighter escorts. This fleet secretly sailed to Hawaii even as Kichisaburo Nomura, Japanese ambassador to the United States, and Saburo Kurusu, Japan's special envoy, were in talks with Secretary of State Cordell Hull to negotiate the outstanding differences between Japan and the United States and to arrive at a peaceful solution to the looming crisis in the Pacific.

The attack on Pearl Harbor was the opening move by the Imperial Navy in a much wider attack against other installations in the Pacific. In the first 24 hours, the Japanese attacked Hong Kong, Guam, Wake Island, and Midway Island.[2] The Japanese Imperial Army landed on the east coast of the Malay Peninsula with the ultimate aim of attacking Singapore.[3] The Japanese bombed the Philippines just nine hours after the bombs began falling on Pearl Harbor, destroying nearly all of the American P-40 fighters and B-17 bombers, effectively eliminating American airpower in the Far East. This put the Philippines out of reach of the U.S. Navy, laying them wide open to a full-scale Japanese invasion. On 22 December Japanese amphibious forces landed in Lingayen Gulf on the main island of Luzon and quickly secured two airfields to be used as forward bases for the occupation of all the Philippines. MacArthur and his command in Manila withdrew to the island fortress of Corregidor, but Franklin D. Roosevelt ordered MacArthur to leave and proceed to Australia by way of a PT boat. Only with great reluctance did he comply with this order on 12 March 1942, promising, "I shall return." Bataan fell on 9 April, and Gen. Jonathan Wainwright formally surrendered Corregidor and the rest of the Philippines on 6 May after a final assault by 2,000 Japanese troops.

These attacks almost destroyed the U.S. Pacific Fleet, and even if the United States could recover, it no longer had any forward bases from which to launch an effective counterattack.

By February 1942, Japan reigned supreme and unchallenged across 122° of longitude and over millions of square miles of the western Pacific and Southeast Asia. Australia was threatened with invasion. It would be three long, grueling years before the U.S. military recaptured the Philippines and the other islands of the Central Pacific from which it could threaten Japan with invasion.

Why did the Japanese attack the United States and plunge itself into a war that some in the Imperial government thought it could not win? Since the early 1930s Japan had initiated the policies of the Greater East Asia Co-Prosperity Sphere, designed to subjugate the region to the glory and benefit of Japan. Just as Hitler had envisaged Russia as Lebensraum for an expanding German population, the Japanese invaded and occupied Manchuria and coastal China, intending to settle 5 million Japanese there within 20 years. Also, by the turn of the century, Japan had become a net importer of food. Until then it had never been dependent on the outside world.

Now Japan had to import more and more from the United States and from territories controlled by the West. It was almost totally dependent on oil imports to fuel its military-industrial complex. But the deeper Japan became involved in the quagmire in China, the more dependent it became on the United States and European possessions in Southeast Asia for raw materials, oil, and food. Accordingly, Japan's military leaders, who were unquestionably dictating foreign policy, set out to make Japan self-sufficient.

One response would be to cut their losses and withdraw from an unwinnable struggle in China. But this would have meant losing face. Expansion was seen as the prerequisite for self-sufficiency.

For its growing list of war crimes perpetrated on China, most notably the strategic bombing of the civilian population in Canton, Roosevelt called for a "moral embargo" of Japan of American exports, especially of arms and the means to manufacture them. This was the first expression of American displeasure with Japan.

In July 1940, Roosevelt, under the new National Defense Act, banned exports of aviation fuel and some other special petroleum products just as huge Japanese orders had been placed for these items to meet their growing needs for ongoing operations in China. Fearing that the United States would make full use of its economic leverage to save its diplomatic position in China, Japan turned covetous eyes on the mineral-rich Dutch, French, and British territories in Southeast Asia.

The army opportunists in Tokyo turned the Japanese fully around to the southern strategy in June 1940. Still entangled in China, they now risked a two-front war. To their credit, they limited their designs to French Indochina, the Dutch East Indies (present-day Indonesia), and British possessions, leaving out all American territories including the Philippines. They were gambling that a German defeat of Great Britain would force America to concentrate on the European theater, leaving Japan unchallenged in the Pacific.

The Japanese Imperial Navy countered with the argument that the United States was too closely tied to Great Britain and the Netherlands to just sit idly by and watch Japan gobble up their colonies. The navy further argued that the American military presence in the Philippines, if left untouched, would leave the flank of their southern advance exposed. Rather than run the risk of ignoring the United States, Japan needed to consider the much greater risk of attacking them.

Roosevelt ordered the Pacific Fleet to move from San Diego to Pearl Harbor in May 1940 to deter Japanese expansion in the Pacific. At the same time, the Netherlands and France fell to the German blitzkrieg, effectively taking them out of the world military equation and allowing Japan to turn its unchallenged attention on the Dutch East Indies and French Indochina.

It fell to Adm. Isoroku Yamamoto, who had lived in Washington as senior naval attaché in 1926–28, to plan the attack on the American fleet now stationed at Pearl Harbor. His rationale was simple: once Japan had conquered the mineral-rich Indies, it would need a defensive perimeter large enough to protect them and the Japanese Home Islands from attack. This perimeter would be more secure and Japan would have gained much needed time to further consolidate its military position only if the U.S. Navy, the only credible threat in the region, could be crippled at the outset.

It should be noted that the planes of the Japanese strike force began dropping bombs and torpedoes on Pearl Harbor seven minutes earlier than scheduled. Tokyo planned to notify Secretary Hull a half hour before hostilities began so that later they could deny any allegation of a sneak attack. The intended gesture was meaningless because an ultimatum with an intended duration of only half an hour is indistinguishable from an undeclared war. But, according to the traditional Bushido code of the Samurai philosophy, all is fair in war–including surprise attacks.

Japan attacked Pearl Harbor because it correctly identified the United States as the only power capable of frustrating its aims in the Pacific and Southeast Asia and because it grossly underestimated the resolve and fighting capability of enraged Americans.

Strategy to Defeat Japan

Adm. Ernest King, chief of naval operations, developed the overall strategy to defeat Japan. Simply put, it was to hold Hawaii, sustain Australasia (Australia, New Zealand, and neighboring South Pacific islands), and as soon as possible drive northwestward against Japanese-held islands and eventually Japan itself. Within this grand strategy, two rival plans emerged to bring about the desired aim, one by the Army and one by the Navy.

Gen. Douglas MacArthur's strategy called for recapturing the Philippines, seizing Okinawa and Formosa (Taiwan) to protect his flanks, and then landing a million troops on the Chinese mainland. From there he would launch the final invasion and conquest of Japan.

Adm. Chester Nimitz envisioned a massive amphibious operation from Okinawa led by the Marines to establish a beachhead on Kyushu, the southernmost island of the Japanese Home Islands.

In the end, these two plans were combined. The Pacific was divided into two theaters of operation. MacArthur was given command of the Southwest Pacific (the Dutch East Indies, the Philippines, Borneo, New Guinea, and Australia). He would drive north to the Philippines along the coast of New Guinea. Nimitz was given command of the Central Pacific and, having stopped the Japanese at Guadalcanal in the Solomons, would drive across the Central Pacific, hopping over a chain of islands including the Gilbert Islands (Tarawa), the Marshall Islands (Kwajalein and Roi-Namur), Guam, the Marianas (Saipan and Tinian), and Iwo Jima to Okinawa.

Control of the skies over Japan and the thousands of miles of sea lane approaches to it was essential to the success of the eventual invasion of Japan from either China or Okinawa. In preparation, military planners envisaged several months of saturation bombing of Japanese industrial centers and military installations. To do this required the use of a large bomber and the beginning of the Very Long-Range (VLR) bomber program conceived by Gen. Henry H. "Hap" Arnold of the Army Air Forces.

As early as May 1941, the Boeing Aircraft Company had been commissioned to design and build the B-29 Superfortress. The B-29 had a range of 3,500 miles and could carry a bomb load of four tons, surpassing the B-17's 2,400 miles and two-ton bomb load. It had a cruising speed of 350 mph and, because it had a pressurized cabin, could fly at an altitude of over 30,000 feet.

By the summer of 1944 the Marianas and Guam had been captured. With these islands secure, the United States had penetrated the inner defensive perimeter guarding the seaborne approaches to Japan. Within weeks the Army Corps of Engineers and the Navy Construction Battalions (Seabees) had begun hacking out the jungle and paving runways three miles long on the three islands capable of handling the large number of B-29s.

From the Marianas the B-29s began large-scale bombing of the Japanese Home Islands. The 3,000-mile roundtrip was hazardous, resulting in heavy losses to antiaircraft fire and fighter attacks. Many damaged bombers could not make it back to the Marianas and had to ditch in emergency water landings. Casualties among the bomber crews were so high that Gen. Curtis LeMay, commanding the 20th Air Force, said the losses were unsustainable. Iwo Jima was the reason for the high casualties. It lay along the flight path of the bombers. Radar on Iwo Jima gave Japan a two-hour notice of the incoming raid; time to alert fighters and antiaircraft batteries. Crippled bombers damaged during the raid were particularly vulnerable to Iwo Jima–based fighters during the return trip. The 1,500-mile flight to Japan stretched the fuel limit of the bombers, which left little time over the targets, decreasing their effectiveness. Additionally, Japanese fighters on Iwo Jima made almost nightly raids on the Marianas airfields, destroying many B-29s on the ground. As long as Japan controlled Iwo Jima, it posed a threat to the success of the bombing campaign.

Iwo Jima was the only island between the Marianas and Japan where airfields could be built to handle the large B-29s. Instead of serving as an early warning station for the Japanese, Iwo Jima could be a haven for damaged B-29s and for those short on fuel and as a forward base for American fighter escorts for the bombers. It would also secure the eastern flank of the proposed invasion of the Japanese Home Islands. U.S. military strategic planners knew it was essential to take Iwo Jima.

2

Growing Up in Indiana

A cold winter wind blew across the campus from the recently harvested cornfields that surround West Lafayette, Indiana, home of Purdue University. The 1941 fall semester at Purdue was winding down, and the men of Sigma Chi fraternity were looking forward to going home for Christmas in two weeks.

The Purdue Boilermakers had recently lost the Old Oaken Bucket game, the last football game of the season, to Indiana University, 7-0. Indiana would have bragging rights for a year and get to keep the Bucket, with its long chain of *I*s and *P*s signifying the most recent winner, until the end of the next season. It is a game that has little meaning to those outside the state of Indiana, but for those who are blessed to call themselves Hoosiers it is really more than just another Saturday afternoon game. Years later, bumper stickers on some cars at Purdue read: "Hoosier by birth; Boilermaker by the grace of God." It is such a fierce rivalry that, for Purdue and Indiana students, the Bucket game is tantamount to war itself. Fistfights had been known to erupt between Purdue and IU fans after football and basketball games. At the time, there was a real war raging in Europe. But that war, an ocean away, was less on the minds of Purdue students, lazily sitting around the Sigma Chi house, than was the upcoming holiday break.

The Sigma Chi fraternity house stood on a hill overlooking the Wabash River. Jim Craig, a skinny freshman from Pendleton, Indiana, sat on the floor of a room they called the library (even though it contained no books), reading the school newspaper. A crackling fire in the fireplace warmed the room from the howling wind while a radio in the corner droned on with relaxing background music. It was Sunday morning, 7 December 1941.

The radio announcement that Pearl Harbor had been attacked would forever change Jim's life. Three years later, his courage and leadership skills would be put to the supreme test. He would come to understand the sublime concept of duty, honor, and sacrifice during one of America's darkest hours, and he would do so in the crucible of mortal combat on a tiny volcanic Pacific island called Iwo Jima.

—··—

James Richard Craig was born in May 1923 to Sydney and Kathryn Craig in Noblesville, Indiana, a little town in Hamilton County just north of Indianapolis. His great-grandfather, a Scottish Presbyterian minister, had moved there from Merryville, Tennessee. When Jim was two years old, his family moved to a 60-acre farm his grandfather owned just north of Durbin, Indiana, between Lapel and Noblesville on SR 32. In 1932 his father purchased half interest in a tomato canning factory in Pendleton, a small town in Madison County northeast of Indianapolis. Two years later, he bought a rundown house at the corner of Broadway and High Street in Pendleton.

Jim attended a two-room school in Durbin before his family moved to Pendleton. Although he spent his freshman and sophomore years at Pendleton High School, his father did not think that the local school system offered a curriculum in science and math up to his standards. He mentioned this to a friend in the canning business, Paul Wolf, who was a Quaker. At the time the Quakers were known to run co-educational boarding schools of high repute. Paul suggested that Syd consider Westtown, a Quaker boarding school located just outside West Chester, Pennsylvania, near Philadelphia. Knowing that money spent on a good, sound education was money well spent, Syd enrolled Jim and Syd Jr. at Westtown.

Located on the beautiful rolling hills of eastern Pennsylvania, the Westtown campus consisted of an eighteenth-century brick building, a picturesque lake, several soccer fields, and a baseball diamond. Classrooms were on the first floor of the main building. At each end of the first floor was a room called the "Collections" where the students gathered for morning prayers, one for the boys and one for the girls. The dormitory rooms were located on the second and third floors; the boys' rooms were judiciously separated from the girls' rooms by some teachers' apartments.

Jim went to Westtown in 1939 just as Germany launched its invasion of Poland, plunging Europe into a continental war. Germany quickly overran Belgium, Holland, and France, began the bombing blitz over London, and invaded Russia. In just over two years the German occupation stretched from the Atlantic coast to the suburbs of Moscow.

Many American newspapers, especially those owned by William Randolph Hearst, supported isolationism, and isolationism was preached at Westtown, with its pacifist Quaker mentality. At the time there was no concern at Westtown about the possibility of war with Japan, although a war with Germany that would involve America was a disconcerting possibility.

During the summer, Jim returned to Pendleton and worked at his father's canning factory, assisting the bookkeepers. Every Friday, the bookkeeper and Jim went down to the local bank and filled envelopes with the employees' wages, to be distributed the following morning.

Jim made extra money by running a concession business at the plant. He bought candy and soft drinks from a local wholesaler and sold them to the canning employees. He quickly developed a keen business acumen, which would serve him well after the war. When he was not helping the bookkeeper, he was peddling his drinks and candy. If a worker did not have any money to pay for the snacks, Jim would mark it in a notebook. Since he was the bookkeeper's assistant, he had direct access to employees' pay and could deduct what he was owed. He made these rounds several times a day. In this way he was able to bring in an additional $40–45 per week. Jim thought he was rich. One day his father had to fire someone who owed Jim candy and pop money. Jim had to write off the loss.

During winter vacations Jim helped in the warehouse. At age 16, when he was able to drive, he helped deliver cases to wholesale groceries in Anderson, Marion, and Indianapolis. But his snack concession remained the more lucrative job.

When Jim was a freshman in high school, his mother enrolled him in a dance course at the Arthur Jordan Conservatory of Music in Indianapolis. Most boys his age would recoil from such an activity, but Jim developed quite a passion for tap dancing. He seemed to have a natural aptitude and rhythm for dance. His idol was Fred Astaire, and he tried to pattern his movements on those of the great master. Occasionally Jim and his class put on reviews for the parents at Shortridge High School in Indianapolis.

Unfortunately, time devoted to dancing conflicted with a sport that comes quite naturally to Hoosier boys, and true to his Hoosier heritage, Jim dearly wished to play basketball for Pendleton High. He tried out for the school team during his freshman year, but his small stature ruled out a basketball career. He continued the dance classes during his sophomore year. He now attributes his survival on Iwo Jima partly to the nimbleness and agility he acquired in his dance classes, which allowed him to quickly maneuver around the battlefield as bullets and mortar shells landed all around him, and to his small size, which presented a smaller target to Japanese snipers.

Jim enrolled at Purdue University in 1941. Because of the war in Europe and East Asia, he took Army Reserve Officers Training Corps (ROTC) classes. It was not a requirement, but it was expected of all incoming male students. He joined Sigma Chi fraternity.

During his junior year, Jim served as one of eight junior vice presidents on the Student Union Board, an organization dedicated to student campus activities. As one of the vice presidents he was in charge of a group of students. A pretty freshman from the Pi Beta Phi sorority house caught his attention. Pat Carroll of Knightstown, Indiana, and her friend Dottie Dodderidge were assigned to Jim's group. These groups regularly rotated to other student vice presidents. Pat had also noticed Jim, and when her group rotated, she left it and returned to his. They went to campus dances, and Pat attended Jim's intramural softball games. One day after a game he asked her if she would like to go to a movie to which she readily agreed. They walked across town to the Mars Theater in Lafayette, where they watched the new Disney animated movie *Bambi*. Jim was smitten.

When Jim and his fraternity brothers first heard about the Japanese attack on Pearl Harbor, they didn't know what it meant. None of them had ever heard of Pearl Harbor. Shortly after Japan officially declared war on the United States, Adolf Hitler followed with his own declaration of war. Jim listened to President Roosevelt's "Day of Infamy" speech on the radio the next day.

Several of Jim's older fraternity brothers who were ROTC officers quickly received orders to ship out for advanced training at Army bases before deployment to the European theater. Jim knew that it was only a matter of time before he, too, would be called up.

For the foreseeable future Jim was not likely to be drafted into the Army because of his status as a student. There was also a long lag period after Pearl Harbor before the United States military could gear itself up to handle the tens of thousands of young men who immediately enlisted. The existing training facilities were inundated with new recruits. It also took time to retool American industrial might for wartime production. Jim knew he would serve in some branch of the service, but he didn't want to serve in the infantry. He considered the Army Air Corps, the Navy, and the Marines. In December 1943 he walked over to the Marine Corps recruiting office in Lafayette to ask about joining. He thought he would look good in Marine dress blues.

Within days he was told to report to the Kresge Building in Indianapolis. On a cold Sunday morning, Jim was sworn in and given an induction physical exam. Many of his fellow enlistees were immediately shipped off to boot camp at Parris Island, South Carolina. The recruiter told Jim to go back to Purdue and continue his education. He was given a registration card to show to the draft board and allowed to stay for two more semesters.

When the Army took over the Sigma Chi house, Jim had to move out. He and other Marine recruits with a deferment status moved into another fraternity house taken over by the Navy. He continued to attend classes, but now he wore a uniform and associated with other recruits. He was given the temporary rank of private, but because he was a college student he was earmarked for Officer Candidate School (OCS) following basic training at boot camp.

One weekend Jim and his dad took the train down to Montgomery, Alabama, to visit Syd Jr., who was training with the Army Air Corps. The barracks there were nice and clean. Jim wore his Marine dress blue uniform during his visit, and to his surprise, the Army recruits began saluting him. This struck him as strange because he was only a private and one only saluted an officer. He figured that because of his spiffy uniform they all thought he must be an officer, hence the deferential treatment. He felt somewhat uncomfortable with this misplaced attention, but he returned the salutes anyway. It was good practice.

3

Platoon Leader

> For the strength of the Pack is the Wolf, and the
> strength of the Wolf is the Pack.
> —Rudyard Kipling, *Second Jungle Book*

Boot Camp, MCRD, Parris Island, S.C.

At the end of 1943, Jim and several of his friends finally received orders to report to the Marine Corps Recruiting Depot at Parris Island in South Carolina. Late in the evening of 13 January 1944, they boarded a train in Lafayette. Only uniformed Marine recruits were on board. The train coaches were specifically designed for troop transport, not for comfort, and Jim nearly froze that night.

They proceeded to Cincinnati where the engine was disconnected and another engine hooked on for the trip to South Carolina. It was very cold in Cincinnati as they were marched into Union Station where they received some breakfast and a hot, welcome cup of joe. Jim was already learning the Marine lexicon. To Marines, a cup of joe was a cup of coffee. In the coming weeks he would learn a whole new set of terms and phrases. After an overnight ride, he and his fellow recruits arrived at Yamisee, the last civilian town before Parris Island. Here they disembarked and walked across the street, through some barricades, and entered the camp, a sprawling 7,819-acre spread of towering moss-draped oak trees and stubby palmettos infested with thousands of rattlesnakes and millions of mosquitoes. Once past this barricade, life would never be the same for Jim. He turned his back on the comforts and ease of civilian life and entered the rigors and discipline of military life. He was about to begin a grueling, time-tested process in which he would be transformed from a skinny young man into a hardened and disciplined Marine.

Discipline was essential. According to the May 1944 *Headquarters Bulletin*, "Too often 'discipline' is interpreted by the untrained individual as a restriction of his personal rights and privileges, rather than as a highly necessary and often life-saving factor in his military education. Without discipline, troops in combat would be a rabble, readily routed by a well-trained, disciplined opponent. . . . Once discipline becomes second nature to the individual, his training progress speeds up and his safety in battle becomes greater." Success in the Pacific during World War II is often attributed to superior Marine discipline. It was essential to the prompt and proper execution of orders in the face of withering gunfire. Eventually recruits got to the point when they reacted to orders without questioning them; it became automatic. It was this kind of discipline that kept men moving forward off the beaches on Iwo Jima when all hell was breaking loose around them; with bullets flying past so close you could hear them; with mortar shells crashing down on them; and with comrades being blown to bits.

Boot camp was the first step whereby individuals were completely broken down and rebuilt into fighting men. The basic tenets included depersonalization, uniforms, lack of privacy, forced social relationships, tight schedules, lack of sleep, and disorientation followed by rites of reorganization according to military codes, arbitrary rules, and strict punishment.[1] In *Iwo Jima: Legacy of Valor*, Bill Ross of the 1st Marine Division defined "the purpose of boot camp: to mold the broadest mix of young Americans into skilled tradesmen in a kill-or-be-killed business, and to keep intact and untarnished the glory and traditions of the United States Marine Corps."

Upon arrival at Parris Island, Jim and the other recruits passed some Marines in full packs marching in the opposite direction. As they passed they heard someone say, "You'll be sorrrrreey." A rough-looking sergeant ordered them to fall in and then, in a thick Southern drawl, offered them a greeting: "Now listen up, you knuckleheads. Your heart belongs to your mother, your soul belongs to Jesus, but your ass belongs to me. You are no longer people. You are not Marines. You are 'boots,' and there ain't nothin' on the evolutionary scale lower than a boot." This sergeant was to be their drill instructor (DI), and he would be at the center of their lives for the next ten weeks. He would be the source of their frustration and the man they most often hated, but they would later come to appreciate him for his role in shaping them into Marines.

Next they were marched to the finance officer who ordered them to purchase an "optional" $10,000 life insurance policy; the $6.40 premium would be deducted from their monthly pay. Jim never saw his pay during boot camp; it just accumulated in an account for him. They were told to fill in the name of a beneficiary—"wife, mother, sister, whore, whoever."

In the process of transforming a boot into a Marine, the first step is to strip away all vestiges of civilian life and individuality. This process began with the haircut. Jim got in line with other boots at the base barbershop like so many sheep awaiting the shearer. With a few swipes of the shears he and the rest of the boots were shorn.

They were given another physical by Navy corpsmen. Standing in a long line with other recruits, Jim received immunization shots in both arms simultaneously. He was poked and examined and finally declared fit.

The next stop was the quartermaster's warehouse, where he was issued his gear. At the first station he was handed a seabag, in which he carried his gear and personal belongings when he traveled from one posting to another. At the next station he received his skivvies, including four sets of green boxer shorts and high-neck T-shirts. (It had been noted early in the war that white underwear made an easy target for snipers, so underwear was dyed olive drab.) Next came shirts and trousers. They were reminded that Marines wore trousers and women wore pants.

Moving on, he was issued an M1 rifle, a backpack, two canteens, a first aid kit, a web cartridge belt, and two pairs of shoes, one for dress, the other (boondockers) for regular use. He was also given a galvanized scrub bucket, two bars of Ivory soap, and a heavy-duty brush for daily laundry chores.

He was assigned to a platoon of about 45 others who, because of their college education, were designated as officer candidates. Their training was essentially the same for all boots, although Jim thought the DIs were a little harder on future officers. Otherwise, they marched, drilled, and trained like everybody else. They were all lowly recruits.

He shared his living quarters, a Quonset hut, with seven other boots, some of whom he knew from Purdue. His personal space consisted of a cot and a footlocker, which also served as a chair. After all, no one would dare sit on a cot once it had been made. If a cot were not perfectly made, without a single wrinkle, one could expect an invective tirade of four-letter words from the DI, who would tear it up and order the hapless boot to remake it. It had to look perfect with sheets and blanket neatly tucked in. Like the uniform he wore, his bed linen had to have absolutely no wrinkles in it. His newly issued clothes went into the footlocker, and the bucket and brush went under the cot. Every recruit's place in the barracks had to look exactly like all the other recruits. There was no place for any individuality in the Marine Corps; by design they were all the same.

The grounds in front of the barracks had to be raked clean so that the sand had little ridges from the rake. The inside of the barracks had to be even cleaner. This was done by what came to be called "holy stoning the decks." Everything was taken out of the barracks, and the floor was cleaned by pouring sand and water on it and scrubbing it with bricks. It was not unusual for Jim to end up with raw knuckles. After they had "holy stoned" the deck, they washed all the sand out the door. Once everything was cleaned and put back in its proper place, they stood at attention for inspection. If their DI did not like what he saw, they were made to do it all over again.

All of this—arrival, greeting by the DI, haircut, issuance of gear, and assignment to a barracks—took place during the morning of the first day of boot camp. At 1145 they were ordered to fall in and march to the mess hall. Here Jim learned Marine table manners. His eating personal space was limited to 18 inches, the width of his metal mess tray.

After lunch they received instructions from the DI on the proper way of folding clothes and placing them in the footlocker. Everything was arranged in strict accordance with the *Guidebook for Marines*, which each boot was required to purchase from the Post Exchange. This was a red manual that contained regulations and the eleven General Orders governing conduct and the chain of command, highlights of Marine Corps history, and the deeds of its legendary heroes.

At 2200 taps was played over the public address system and the lights were turned out. Jim had survived his first day of boot camp.

The transformation had begun. In subtle ways, the recruits were being set apart from the rest of society. It was this indoctrination through which the boots came to embody the tradition of the Marine Corps known as esprit de corps, that sense of unity which develops among those who are closely associated in a cause.

Leon Uris defined the Marines' esprit de corps in his 1953 book, *Battle Cry*: "In a way it's love. I mean, you love these people. You're there to share a moment. There was enormous love between these guys. You absolutely knew the guy next to you was going to come through for you. It was a reminder of one's duty to the Corps and to each other, a selfless giving of one's life, if necessary, for his buddies."

In *Iwo Jima: Legacy of Valor*, Bill Ross wrote: "Membership in the *corps d'elite* was to them [Marines] the highest possible calling as rugged individuals whose first duty was to the Marine Corps . . . then to God and country." In his Marine Corps memoir, *Goodbye, Darkness*, William Manchester wrote: "Men, I now know, do not fight for flag or country, for the Marine Corps or glory or any other abstraction. They fight for one another. Any man in combat who lacks comrades who will die for him, or for whom he is willing to die, is not a man at all. He is truly damned."

War correspondent Robert Sherrod wrote: "From the time he underwent the severe discipline of 'boot' camp, until he died assaulting a Japanese pillbox, the Marine had it drummed into his head: 'You are the best fighting man on earth, and you'd better never do anything to disprove it.' His training included not only a thorough course in the use of weapons but also a stiff indoctrination . . . [in] 'moral superiority.'"[2]

It was in this environment of deep and abiding tradition and esprit de corps that Jim Craig found himself that first day at Parris Island. It was here and later in more advanced training that he and his fellow Marines developed, through hard work and shared suffering, a love for one another, a devotion to duty, and a higher calling of service.

———·—·———

Reveille sounded in the cold predawn darkness each morning at 0400, rousting the boots from a sound sleep. Thus began an 18-hour day of nearly constant activity, of unremitting prodding and harassment from the DI. Once out of bed, Jim had 10 minutes to relieve himself, shave, dress in the prescribed uniform of the day, and make his bed. He was allotted 20 minutes for breakfast, which consisted of a ladle of grits and a ladle of baked beans, and then 10 minutes to square away his barracks for inspection before mustering for roll call. Everything was regimented according to a strict, demanding schedule.

When his platoon was ordered to fall out, they were never quite fast enough to satisfy their DI. He would have them go back and do it again, yelling as they hustled back to the barracks, "I don't wanna see nothin' but heels and assholes. So get going and do it right this time."

The first formal activity of the day was 45 minutes of rigorous calisthenics followed by close order drill. The DI sang to the rhythm of their marching cadence with a lilting chant. Although Jim and his fellow officer candidates were well versed in drill from their NROTC training in college, the DI heaped curses on them with every step. The morning's activities ended with a run to the mess hall for lunch.

The afternoon brought no let up. It was packed with rigorous training in the use of the bayonet and hand-to-hand combat scuffling—the more strenuous and savage, the better. This brutal training was designed for a specific purpose: survival in combat and to develop a kill-or-be-killed mentality on the battlefield. Three DIs, a sergeant and two corporals, screamed, cursed, and threatened the often scared recruits with dire consequences if they did not slug each other with greater violence. For this Jim often swore right back at the DI under his breath. He also learned to crawl under barbed wire with live machine gun bullets zinging just over his head. It was pounded into him to keep his heels turned down so that they would not be shot off. Attention to details like this saved lives on the beaches in the Pacific.

Regardless of the job a Marine was eventually assigned—a cook, a mechanic, or a grunt in the infantry—all Marines were riflemen. In addition to any specialized training they received, they had to become proficient with the rifle.

After a few weeks of boot camp, Jim and his platoon were marched out to the rifle range. He carried all the gear he would need in his seabag and lived for a week with his fellow boots in a barracks near the range.

Before heading out to the rifle range, the DI demonstrated the proper way to care for an M1 Garand rifle. A dirty rifle might misfire or jam, so the DI labored the point of keeping the rifle clean. This was just as important to the rifleman as shooting it. It was to become his best friend, and he was never to lose it. After all, what good is a rifleman without a rifle?

Jim learned to strip down and reassemble his rifle until he could do it blindfolded. At any time he might be pulled aside and required to recite the serial number of his rifle and demonstrate its proper use. Occasionally Jim was asked to do this, and he never had any trouble passing the test. "Yes, sir. This is my .30-caliber, gas operated, clip-fed, air-cooled, semiautomatic M1 rifle, serial no. 532989, sir." To this day he still remembers his rifle's serial number.

Before learning to use the M1 rifle, they took some practice shots with a .22-caliber rifle. Once they had become used to the sound and feel of shooting a rifle, they were given their M1 Garand, the main weapon of a Marine rifleman.[3]

All boots had to learn to fire from three positions: sitting, prone, and standing. When they were learning to fire from the sitting position, the drill instructor came around to each boot to make suggestions. Sometimes his suggestion was more than just a comment. If he thought someone was not sitting low enough, he would mash down on his head to remind him to keep it down. This may seem a little harsh, but everything the DI did was intended to increase the chances a Marine would survive combat. A head that stuck up too high was a tempting target for a Japanese sniper, and many Marines were killed because they did not keep low enough to the ground.

The first time Jim fired his M1 rifle, he thought it had exploded, but he got used to the feel and sound of it. Targets were placed 600 yards away, the maximum effective range of the M1. He practiced the three positions, but found firing while seated the most difficult. They each fired when ready, so there was a constant din. At the other end of the rifle range, another boot behind a protective berm raised a stick with a red sign indicating that the target was missed completely. When a boot missed the target, it was said that he had shot "Maggie's Drawers." One of the first times that Jim fired his rifle from 600 yards, he hit a bull's-eye, but the next time he shot "Maggie's Drawers." Another time he shot a bull's-eye but was shown "Maggie's Drawers." When he looked carefully, he realized that he had hit the wrong target.

Punishment was meted out to the sorry boot with a dirty rifle and even worse if he dropped it, but woe to the boot who committed the unforgivable sin of referring to it as a gun. Jim did drop his rifle once, and the punishment was swift. A common punishment for this offense was to have to sleep with the rifle. The cot that Jim slept in was just wide enough for him, so to sleep with his rifle was uncomfortable. The DI came around in the night to make sure Jim was still sleeping with it. Through this experience he learned to take good care of his rifle.

There were other forms of punishment meted out by the DIs for this slip or that mistake. Additional drill, more marching, more pushups, holding a bucket of sand at arm's length until one's arms screamed with pain, and having the DI yell in a boot's face, nose to nose. Another favorite form of punishment, and one designed to embarrass the boot in order to teach him a lesson, was to make him wear his wash bucket over his head. Although some in his platoon had to suffer this indignity, Jim did not.

The DI carried a swagger stick, a hard wooden shaft with a leather handle and polished shell casing at the top. If a boot were caught holding his rifle with his thumb not tucked in properly, he would receive a whack on the thumb with the stick. It was said that there were three ways to do things: the right way, the wrong way, and the Marine way. Jim was learning to do things the Marine way.

Endurance and strength training did not let up at the rifle range. They continued to perform calisthenics and did hundreds of push-ups with the DI standing by to make sure they did them correctly. Another form of endurance training took place in the evenings. The boots were required to hold their full seabags in their outstretched arms and to hold them there at the pleasure of the DI. Jim was not as big as some of the others in his platoon, but he had to carry the same amount of gear and hold it just as long as the rest. He held it until he thought he could not hold it any longer, but he did not dare let it drop even one inch. If a boot let down his bag too soon, the penalty was swift. The DI would take the bag and swing it with all his might into the hapless boot's chest, knocking him off his feet. Holding the seabag was not punishment; everybody did it to build strength. Letting it drop too early was the sin, and getting whacked with it was the punishment.

Another endurance test was holding the 10-pound rifle at arm's length. They were required to hold it for 15 and sometimes 20 minutes. Again, this was not punishment. These kinds of exercises, though they may seem cruel, were meant to toughen up a boot, to get him ready for the rigors of combat. Jim would come to appreciate this training later when he was on the beaches and in the rocky ravines of Iwo Jima.

Finally the day arrived for the men to be qualified in one of three ratings: expert, sharpshooter, or marksman. If a boot did not qualify at one of these ratings, he was required to go through the training all over again. He could not become a Marine without qualifying with the M1 rifle at least to the marksman level. It was a little windy on the day that Jim was to shoot for record, but he qualified as a marksman.

Although neither Germany nor Japan used it during the war, the possible use of gas as an offensive weapon always haunted military planners. Therefore, Jim was issued a gas mask and was trained in its use. In order to learn to don his mask quickly and to get used to the idea of wearing one, he was made to run through buildings filled with noxious but otherwise harmless gas.

Slowly but surely, Jim and his fellow boots were transformed into Marines. It showed in their marching. He could overhear new recruits comment on how well they marched. He still swore under his breath at his DI, but he began to see the value of his methods and harsh treatment. He had developed a pride in himself and the Corps and a confidence that can only come with hard work and discipline. He had learned an all-for-one-and-one-for-all mentality through disciplined teamwork, the foundation upon which the Marine Corps rested.

A proud moment in Jim's life was the completion of boot camp at Parris Island when he was promoted to private first class (PFC). He was ready for the next stage in his training.

Camp Lejeune—Becoming an Officer

Jim completed boot camp at Parris Island on 1 April 1944 and was immediately sent to Camp Lejeune, North Carolina. He was waiting to go to Quantico, Virginia, for Officer Candidate School (OCS), but he had to wait until an opening became available.

As soon as he arrived at Camp Lejeune, he was assigned KP duty for a week. It was not very demanding work and only required him to get up a little earlier than the rest of his buddies. After the first day of KP duty he noticed something about the other Marines that disturbed him. They dragged themselves in for chow early in the morning looking like death warmed over. Their haggard faces stunned him. He wondered what had happened to them.

He soon learned. Every other night they went out on an 18-mile hike carrying a full pack. Eventually Jim was relieved of KP, and he, too, began taking these long hikes. For a good portion of the hike, the terrain was sandy—not the best surface for hiking. It was exhausting work. After about an hour of hiking, the platoon leader called for a 10-minute rest. It was not long before the Marines decided that they would just as soon forgo the ten-minute rest stop and keep going, the sooner to get it over with. It was not long before Jim, too, was dragging himself back to the chow line.

On alternate nights they went out for the compass march. They were taken out at night in trucks and dropped off in the middle of the woods and mosquito-infested swamps with only a map, a compass, and each other to find their way back to camp. The only way to stay together in the pitch dark was to hold onto the rifle of the guy in front. There really was no way to find their way in the dark. After a while they gave up and just sat down and waited until it was light enough to see where they were, then they made their way back into camp. The purpose of this exercise was not so much to teach map and compass reading skills as it was to teach the Marines how to deal effectively with desperate situations.

The Marine Corps was preparing them for the most harrowing and frightening of experiences—mortal combat. They were subjected to everything the Corps could think of to get them as ready as possible. Jim thought training at Camp Lejeune was actually physically tougher than boot camp had been.

Much time was devoted to running through the obstacle course, scaling eight-foot walls, swinging over a mud hole on a rope, and maneuvering over and around other more imaginative barriers. The obstacle course simulated combat conditions. They had to run through a field pocked with shell holes. To get them used to the sounds of combat, sticks of dynamite were planted near the holes and detonated as they ran by.

A log suspended by a rope at each end had been placed across a stream. After much trial and error, Jim had it timed so that if he ran at the stream at just the right speed and angle he could get two steps on the log and make it across without falling in. It was tough by design, and on a few occasions he did slip and fall in the stream. They also practiced disembarkation procedures from assault landing craft on a beach while planes strafed them with live ammunition.

Jim learned to fire .30-caliber (both air- and water-cooled) and .50-caliber machine guns, use a flamethrower, fire an antitank bazooka, set up and fire mortars, and fix and arm demolition charges to blow up bunkers and caves. Others in his company would become experts with specific weapons, but Jim, earmarked for officer training, had to become familiar with all of them. This training reflected experience gained by the Marines fighting the Japanese in earlier Pacific island campaigns such as Guadalcanal and in the central Solomons.

Of these weapons, Jim got the biggest kick from firing a bazooka. He liked to blow things up. Obsolete tanks and jeeps served as practice targets. A bazooka is a two-man weapon.[4] While Jim held the bazooka on his shoulder and aimed at the target through the sights, the second man loaded the round in the rear of the tube. When the round was loaded and ready to be fired, the loader tapped Jim on the helmet. He sighted the jeep in the bazooka's cross hairs and fired. With a "whoosh," the round was shot out the front end, and a couple of seconds later the jeep was obliterated.

Over the course of six weeks at Camp Lejeune Jim became leaner and tougher. The 18-mile night hikes no longer left him huffing and puffing.

One morning in mid-July the posted orders for the day said that he was to fall in with others in his platoon at 0900 hours dressed in starched khakis. They were marched over to the camp theater as the camp band played martial music. After they were seated, a grim-faced officer clued them in on what was happening in the war in the Pacific. He told them that because of the high casualties suffered by Marine officers on Tarawa in the Gilbert Islands and Saipan in the Mariana Islands, there was an acute need for rifle platoon leaders. They were told that some of them had been selected for an accelerated officer training program and that the names of those selected were posted at the barracks. Jim checked the list and found his name on it. He immediately began 10 weeks of intensive combat training.

Jim spent every day in the field honing his combat skills. These included digging foxholes, training for amphibious landings, and learning the art of small unit tactical warfare: maneuver, flanking, concealment, advance, and withdrawal as well as the use of artillery and mortar fire in support of the infantry. He and his fellow officer candidates engaged in war games, at times playing the part of the enemy. They practiced combat on beaches, in the woods, and in the swamps.

Because this was an accelerated training program, the course work in Marine Corps history, parade, military law, and protocol was eliminated. The only hot meal of the day was lunch, but because they were always out in the field training, they usually missed it. All they got for their evening meal was cold cuts. Because of this low calorie diet combined with their heavy training regimen, they lost so much weight that when they underwent their exit physical exams before being commissioned, many, including Jim, were declared unfit for combat. When this intensive training period ended, he began to regain some of the lost weight.

On Saturday, 28 September 1944, during a formal ceremony conducted by a high-ranking Marine officer, Jim finally received his commission as a second lieutenant. A newly commissioned officer was customarily granted 10 days of leave before his next assignment. It was during this leave period that Jim and Pat planned to get married, but the Marine Corps had other plans for him. The prosaic excuse was "There's a war on, you know." The day after his commissioning he boarded a train for a five-day trip to Camp Pendleton for further training.

Camp Pendleton—Becoming a Leader

Camp Pendleton is located north of San Diego along a barren stretch of beach and sand dunes. A bulldozer had carved out an area where tent camps had been set up, and it was at one of these campsites that Jim now found himself. The tent, which he shared with three other officers, had no deck, no lights, no electricity, and no hot water. There was one phone they all shared that was kept in a little concrete hole in the ground. Because there was no electricity, Jim and his tentmates read and wrote letters at night by candlelight.

Half of his new training day was devoted to reading. He learned a little about military law and some of the other things he had missed at Camp Lejeune. Part of the bookwork covered weapons and battlefield tactics. In the afternoons he was back in the field putting into practice some of the things he learned from the books. More time was spent in tactical warfare training similar to what he had learned at Camp Lejeune. He honed the skills he would need to lead a rifle platoon. Boot camp at Parris Island taught him the discipline he needed to become a Marine. At Camp Lejeune he learned what was necessary to become an officer. At Camp Pendleton he practiced the leadership and tactical skills he would need to take men into combat to secure an objective.

There was no set period that Jim and his fellow officers were to spend training at Pendleton. They were in limbo waiting to be assigned to a particular Marine outfit for the next planned campaign in the Pacific. At Pearl Harbor, Adm. Chester W. Nimitz was planning the invasion of Iwo Jima, but Jim and his fellow officers at Pendleton knew nothing of this. They continued to train for the next stage on the road to defeating Japan, whenever and wherever it was.

Not a day went by that Jim did not think about Pat. It had been months since he had last seen her. He longed to talk with her. On the first weekend after arriving at Pendleton, he hitched a ride to Los Angeles and entered a hotel to make a long-distance telephone call. Apparently many other people had the same idea because the lines were busy and he was unable to get through. Love-struck Jim was not deterred. He waited beside the phone in the lobby all afternoon until he could get through. Finally, at 6:00 PM a line cleared, but, as luck would have it, Pat was not home. Dejected, he went back to camp with his friends.

The next evening while he was standing in the chow line a friend ran up and asked, "Did you get the call?" Irritably, Jim asked, "What call? I didn't get any call." His friend said he was wanted on the phone. He had no idea who might be calling him, and he had to decide whether he was going to lose his place in the long chow line to see who was calling him or stay in line. He shrugged and went to the camp phone. He picked it up, identified himself, and was told there was somebody on the line for him. Impatiently, he waited while the operator checked to see if the circuit was still open. A few minutes went by and Jim finally heard Pat's voice. After the usual endearments that lovers whisper to each other, Pat said she was going to come out to visit him. She would be staying with her Uncle Bill and Aunt Edna Roberts, who lived in Long Beach just up the coast from Camp Pendleton. Jim was elated, but before he hung up he stammered a little, then said, "Wait a minute. Do you want to, well, you know, get married?"

There was a pause from the other end, then, "Well, yeah. When do you want to get married? I'm flying out on Wednesday."

"Well, this is Sunday. Why not next Saturday."

"Okay." It was settled.

The next few days passed quickly for Jim as he was engrossed in training. The Marines did not give him time to daydream. Finally Wednesday arrived, and he found a ride to Laguna Beach, halfway between Camp Pendleton and Los Angeles. Uncle Bill met her at the airport and drove her to Laguna Beach. She introduced Jim to Bill, and the three of them had dinner together.

To Jim's great surprise and delight, his father arrived the next day. Bill drove Jim back and forth between Camp Pendleton and Long Beach. This was a time of gas rationing, and how much he could drive was dependent on the number of ration stamps he could get. Bill had to call in some favors from friends and neighbors to get extra ration stamps. It was his contribution to the war effort.

On Friday Bill and Pat took Jim's dad to the camp. After Jim and Pat got the required prenuptial blood test, they took his dad out to see where he had been living. To get to Tent Camp 3 they had to walk through the training fields, through shell holes, and around trenches. They finally reached Jim's tent. One of his tentmates was writing a letter by candlelight. Compared with Syd's barracks in Alabama, Jim's circumstances took him by surprise. That is when it sank in. His son was really in the war now.

On the day of his wedding Jim had to stay in class until noon. He had arranged for a friend to drive him up to Long Beach, but at the last minute the ride fell through; he was stuck at Pendleton with time running out. How was he going to explain this to Pat? As he pondered his situation, his dad and Bill drove up.

Jim and Pat's wedding pictures seem to show a lot of friends in attendance. But the pictures belie the real story. Three weeks earlier, Bill's neighbor was to be married, but the groom got his orders to ship out and the wedding was canceled. Jim and Pat did not know anybody in Long Beach, and since this was, after all, their wedding, Bill and Edna invited all the guests who were to attend the neighbor's wedding to come witness their niece's nuptials. Smartly attired in his new officer's uniform, Jim stood at the bottom of a winding staircase. Pat made her appearance and slowly descended the stairs. When she reached the bottom she took Jim's arm and together they walked into the living room. As a woman sat in a corner playing a harp Jim looked around at all the smiling faces—he did not know a single guest.

Their wedding day was Saturday, 21 October 1944. Nearly four months later, Pat's husband would step out of his landing craft and charge up the volcanic ash-covered beaches of Iwo Jima. In four months she might be a widow. But this was something that Pat never thought much about. Despite the danger, she was sure her husband would come home safely.

After a modest reception, Jim and Pat drove to the Biltmore Hotel in Los Angeles for their honeymoon. The next day Jim's father flew back to Indiana. Bill wanted the young couple to get a good start, so he arranged for them to rent a small place on Balboa Beach—a shack, in Jim's estimation. It was a duplex that they shared with another Marine couple. A Marine friend, Ed Cavalini, lived with his wife in the duplex next door. They stayed there for a week until Uncle Bill found them another place with a little more privacy in Laguna Beach. This would be their home while Jim was in California awaiting orders to ship out. He had no idea how long that would be, but for now he and Pat would take full advantage of what time they had together.

When Jim came home each evening from camp, Pat had dinner waiting. After dinner they went to the beach, sat on the sand, and listened to the surf. Some evenings they had dinner in one of the many little restaurants nearby. Afterwards, they took leisurely walks along the boardwalk. Other evenings they went to bars and listened to local combos. It was an idyllic setting, but on Pacific islands and on the Russian front, soldiers and civilians alike were dying by the thousands. As far as the happy couple was concerned, the war was a million miles away. For what little time they had left together, their little world was dinner in quaint restaurants and walks along the beaches of Southern California holding hands. All that mattered to them was the moment. They were together, and they were in love.

Then Camelot crumbled and the dream ended. On Monday, 20 November 1944, Jim received orders to ship out. He and his fellow officers and replacement Marines were driven down to San Diego, where they boarded a troop ship and set sail. Many who left from the naval base at Coronado Island that day would not return. Pat earnestly prayed that Jim would be one of those who did.

The troop ship sailed north to San Francisco and dropped anchor in the bay. They were not permitted to leave the ship, so Jim and Ed sat on the quarterdeck that night and watched ferryboats ply the waters between San Francisco and Sausalito. The next day they set sail for the Central Pacific. For security reasons it was not until they were well out to sea that they were finally told of their destination—Maui in the Hawaiian Islands. Like most Americans before the 7 December attack, Jim had never heard of Pearl Harbor. Since the attack, everybody knew where Oahu and Pearl Harbor were, but the island of Maui was still unknown to him. Maui would be his home as he began preparing for the amphibious assault on Iwo Jima planned for February.

Life on board ship was a bit more comfortable than at camp. Because of the tradition of segregating officers, Jim was accorded better living accommodations than the enlisted men. He and the other 25 or so officers lived in the officers' quarters. The 200 enlisted men slept in cramped quarters below deck where their bunks were stacked five high, floor to ceiling. It was hot and stuffy below deck, but even the officers did not have the luxury of air-conditioning. Jim ate with the ship's officers in the wardroom where stewards served the meals. They had linen napkins, tablecloths, and silverware. Occasionally Jim overheard some of the enlisted men as they walked past and saw how much better the officers were living and eating. The comments were not complimentary. However, the enlisted men probably didn't know that the officers didn't receive their meals free, as the enlisted men did.

This was Jim's first time on a ship. The seas were a bit rough, but he was spared seasickness. Some of the men could not seem to find their sea legs and had to spend time at the rail. Some got a little green even before the ship left the dock. Jim did not have much in the way of responsibilities en route, so he passed the time reading and playing cards.

One evening Jim and Ed were standing on deck when they noticed one of the other ships of the armada getting awfully close. They watched with incredulity as it continued to bear down on them as if it intended to ram them. Suddenly a stentorian siren began to wail. Men ran around like ants, whereas Jim and Ed continued to watch, transfixed, as the ship bore down on them. At the last moment it swerved, but it got so close that Jim thought he could have reached out and touched it. After the bow passed, they began to worry that the stern might hit them, but that, too, barely missed them. When Jim's pulse returned to normal, he and Ed went below. They had had enough excitement for one evening. The rest of the trip to Hawaii passed without incident.

After a voyage of five days beneath leaden skies, they arrived off the coast of Maui. The scene was unlike anything Jim had ever seen before. It was paradise. A light surf washed onto white sandy beaches, palm fronds swayed in the breeze, and the summit of the extinct volcano, Haleakala, rose majestically in the distance.

Camp Maui—Becoming a Platoon Leader

The Marines disembarked and boarded large military trucks for the ride to Camp Maui, home to the 4th Marine Division. Jim shared a tent with other officers, all of whom were awaiting assignment to a particular unit. At first he was given no responsibilities, no unit to train with. The prevailing rumor—Camp Maui was rife with rumors—was that he and the other newly commissioned second lieutenants would be assigned to beach operations in support of an upcoming campaign, the location and name of which was still a secret. Only the highest echelons of the Marine Corps and Navy knew of the intended objective. He did not know what campaign he was preparing for.

He soon received orders to report to Lt. Col. Alexander A. Vandergrift, commanding officer of the 3rd Battalion, 24th Marines,[5] who was no less than the son of the Marine Corps commandant.

Several junior officers entered Colonel Vandergrift's tent and stood at attention in front of his desk. They removed their caps and stood ramrod straight, with eyes and head fixed straight ahead, chin and stomach in, chest out, and thumbs along the seams of their trousers.

Colonel Vandergrift gave them a pep talk and vaguely described what he expected of them. "You will live, eat, and train with your men. You will become one with them. Now, I know this is your first assignment, but keep in mind, you're in command. Let 'em know right from the beginning who's running the outfit." He then beckoned for Lieutenants Craig, Walker, and Ware to come forward. "I want you three to report to Lieutenant Makowski over at L Company. He's short of rifle platoon leaders. His company took a beating on Saipan, and he needs you as replacements. If there are no questions, you are dismissed." None was expected.

The three went over to Makowski's tent and reported as ordered. Makowski was the commanding officer, or CO, of L Company of the 3rd Battalion, and Lieutenant Young was his executive officer, or XO. Makowski and Young were first lieutenants, one grade rank above Jim, a second lieutenant. Makowski introduced his three new rifle platoon leaders to "Smokey Bear" and "Turkey Hughes," also second lieutenants. "Smokey Bear" commanded the machine gun section, and "Turkey Hughes" commanded the mortar section of the heavy weapons platoon. (Jim never knew their given names.)

After the introductions, Makowski said, "Now listen up. As you know, we're short of rifle platoon leaders, so I'm assigning you to the three platoons of the company. Craig, you've got the 1st platoon, and let me tell you, they're the characters of the company, so work 'em hard and keep 'em in line. Walker, you get the 2nd, and Ware, the 3rd. I suggest you get on over there now and get to know the men under your command."

Lt. Jim Craig, rifle platoon leader of 1st Platoon, L Company, 3rd Battalion, 24th Marines of the 4th Division, left with a smile on his face. He was going to command U.S. Marines. They would be his men. As he made his way to their tents, he reflected on what Makowski had said about his platoon. "They are the characters of the company." What had he meant by that, he wondered. He would find out soon enough.

After introducing himself to the men in his platoon, he had them fall out for a little close order drill so they could start to get used to him. A couple of days later, when they were out on a field exercise, he noticed that several were goofing off. He knew that he had to lay down the law right away. He screwed up his meanest face and yelled, "Halt. Fall in, you knuckleheads." In unison, they did so.

He stood in front of them with his arms akimbo and said in his gruffest voice, "Now I don't give a damn what kind of experience you guys have had or how many campaigns you've been in, but you are going to do this my way and we're going to be out here all day until you get it right. Do I make myself perfectly clear?"

"Yes, sir," they mumbled together.

"What was that? I didn't hear you."

"YES, SIR."

Jim had their attention now, and from that point on he never had any more problems with his men. They marched more smartly and acted more like a cohesive unit. Some of his men had seen action on Roi-Namur, Saipan, and Tinian, where their previous platoon leader had been killed. Others were as new to the platoon as Jim was, but it was not long before they all accepted him as their leader and developed a healthy respect for him.

They were a complete team again. There were 41 men in his platoon, but he quickly learned all their names, nicknames, and idiosyncrasies. Through rigorous training together they gained the confidence they would need to rely on each other in combat.

———·•·———

Ordinarily a Marine rifle platoon in 1944 was composed of a platoon headquarters (HQ) section and three rifle squads. The HQ was composed of a second lieutenant, a platoon sergeant, and five other enlisted men. Each of these enlisted men was armed with an M1 rifle. Each of the three squads, composed of 12 men and a squad sergeant, was divided into three fire teams. A fire team consisted of three privates and a leader who was usually a corporal. Of the three privates on a fire team, two had M1 rifles and one had a BAR. Thus a full strength platoon had nine BARs.

Jim was pleasantly surprised when he was assigned to the 1st Platoon because they had picked up three additional BARs during the battle of Saipan. The BAR (Browning Automatic Rifle) was a .30-caliber automatic rifle that utilized a 20-round magazine. It was essentially a light machine gun that provided more firepower than the standard M1 rifle. This gave his platoon 12 BARs instead of the usual 9, which translated into considerably more firepower.

The three rifle squads of four three-man fire teams gave him a total of 36 men, all privates and corporals. There were three squad sergeants plus one platoon sergeant and one platoon corporal for a total of 41 men. His shortfall was in noncommissioned officers, but he would give up an NCO for an extra BAR any day.

———·•·———

The typical day at Camp Maui started with chow. Jim got up with his men and marched with them to breakfast. He ate with other officers in the officers' mess, and his men ate with other enlisted men in their own mess. The morning was spent in open-air classes reviewing the theory of small unit tactical warfare, and in the afternoon they put the theory into practice. They practiced warfare in wooded gullies near camp, taking turns playing the role of the enemy. Two squads "attacked" while the third squad "defended" a position. He took them out on 14-mile hikes with full packs to get them back into shape after their rest and rehabilitation period following the battles on Saipan and Tinian. During these long marches they were discouraged from drinking a lot of water. The rationale for this was simple. The Marines did not want the men to get used to having as much water as they wanted because there might come a time when water was in short supply. By restricting the water supply it was thought that they would eventually get used to having less or doing without for prolonged periods. This practice was called "water discipline."

Between 27 and 30 November 1944, the three regiments of the 4th Division participated in ship-to-shore landing operations in Maalaea Bay. The surf off the coast of Maui was favorable to this kind of training and was similar to the landing beaches on Iwo Jima. The same kind of Navy troop transports they would use to land on the beaches of Iwo Jima were employed for this training. Once the ships were in position offshore, Jim's platoon climbed over the side and descended to the landing boats on cargo nets. They were taught to use the vertical ropes rather than the horizontal ropes of the net because if one held onto a horizontal rope the man above might step on his hands.

Each landing craft, also referred to as a Higgins boat,[6] held about 30 men, so it took two boats to transport Jim's platoon to the beach. A Navy coxswain maneuvered the boat toward shore but otherwise did not participate in the actual landing.

Once the Marines were all aboard, the coxswain took them out away from the ship and circled while he waited for the other boats. When all the boats were ready, they lined up abreast and proceeded to the beach in a wave. Since this exercise was primarily practice for the Navy, the Marines did not get out. When they hit the beach, the bow of the boat was shoved up and the stern down. A trailing wave following close behind the boat swamped and drenched every man inside, but because the air was so hot and humid, the water was really quite refreshing. Once the boat had beached, the coxswain put it in reverse and went back out to sea to repeat the process. They practiced this landing technique for two days until they had it perfected.

During most of his time on Maui, Jim and his men were isolated and had no access to news about the progress of the war. There were times, however, when an officer returned from the South Pacific and gave a presentation about his experience against the Japanese in previous island campaigns. Attendance at these presentations was required of all officers, and Jim found them both enlightening and sobering. It was his best opportunity to hear from combat veterans who had actually seen and fought the Japanese. It was in one of these talks that Jim first learned about the bloody battle of Tarawa where Marine casualties were very high. He also heard from Marines involved in the battles for Guadalcanal, Bougainville in the Solomon Islands, and Saipan and Tinian in the Marianas.

Even though Jim lived with the men of his platoon, he shared a tent with other officers. His tentmates were "old-timers," veteran junior officers of previous campaigns. At first these officers gave Jim the cold shoulder and refused to speak with him. This puzzled him. As far as he knew, he had done nothing to deserve this treatment. He continued to harbor the thought that it was he who was somehow the reason for their silence until he learned that the other new officers were getting the same treatment. He remained perplexed over this unusual behavior until one of his tentmates pulled him aside and explained.

"Look, Craig, we don't mean to be unfriendly. But you have to understand something about combat. We all lost a lot of good buddies on Saipan and Tinian, guys we'd gotten to know real well. That's the problem, see. You get to know somebody real well one day and, bam, he's dead the next. It's real hard on you. Sometimes it seems like you're just better off not getting too close to somebody for fear that he's going to get killed. So it's nothing you did. Don't take it personal. It's just that we're afraid to lose another buddy. You'll understand what I'm talking about one of these days once you've been in combat."

Jim was moved by this officer's comments. What these veterans were doing by their silence was throwing up a psychological barrier to shield themselves from the pain of losing yet another friend. If they did not make a friend, they would not lose one, so the thinking seemed to go. Psychological isolation was a defense against further hurt.

Once Jim was settled at Camp Maui, he began writing letters to Pat. For security reasons the Marines were under strict orders not to divulge their location in their letters or telephone calls home. Before leaving San Diego, he and Pat had come up with a novel way around this prohibition. They devised a code whereby he could clue her in as to his whereabouts. The last sentence of his letters contained the secret code. To the casual reader this sentence would look innocent enough, but the first letter of key words, when put together, spelled out his location. The key words would be obvious to Pat, but unlikely to anybody else. The first letter he sent her from Hawaii ended: "Please say hello to Mary And Uncle Ike," meaning Maui. This was an egregious breech of security and probably would have been a court-martial offense had the military censors got hold of his letter and broken their code, but he never got caught.

During a rare three-day leave Jim and some of his buddies went to Waikiki Beach and stayed in the Royal Hawaiian Hotel for the day. They changed into their swimming trunks and spent most of the day body surfing, playing paddleball, and lounging in the sun. These respites were welcome diversions from the rigorous training regimen.

As an officer, Jim occasionally got pulled for MP (military police) duty. When he went into town on his designated days with this duty, he wore an MP armband. His job was to ensure that no trouble came between off-duty Marines and the civilian population. Drinking beer at one of the many local bars was a favorite off-duty pastime. As often happens when young Marines drink, some got drunk and became unruly. When a Marine got drunk, the local police picked him up and took him to jail. Jim's last duty at the end of the evening was to drive into town to bring the disorderly Marines back to camp. He usually got a big kick out of this part of the job. It was all he could do to look and sound mad. He would pace up and down in front of the jail cells looking sternly at the forlorn Marines.

"Come on, Lieutenant. Get us out of here," they beseeched.

Jim would pace a little more, then turn and say, "You sons of bitches can all just rot in hell. I ought to just leave you in there."

"Oh, come on, Lieutenant. We didn't hurt no one. We just had a little to drink."

As always, Jim eventually relented and drove them back to base, but not before offering a stern warning: "Okay, just this once. But, if I ever catch you guys in here again, I *will* leave you. Now, come on. Get your sorry asses on the truck, and let's get back to camp."

The training continued unabated for the next few weeks as Jim and the men of the 1st Platoon practiced the art of combat. Along with other platoons, they held little war games, each platoon taking turns playing the enemy. They would go on long marches, then "attack," using blank ammunition.

Admiral Nimitz had long since decided that Iwo Jima would be assaulted in mid-February, now only two months away.[7] Late in December, the pace of training was accelerated. Everything was done to simulate combat conditions.

Jim often reflected on what Colonel Vandergrift had said when he was assigned to the 1st Platoon: "You will live, eat, and train with your men.

You will become one with them." Vandergrift had been right. Jim had done just that, and in the process he had gotten to know every man in his platoon. More important, he knew that they would do what was necessary when the time came to hit the beaches. He was confident that when bullets were zinging everywhere and shells were exploding all around, when men were dying and screaming from horrible wounds, when it seemed they were in hell itself, the training would take over and they would do their duty. They had developed a mutual respect for each other, a kind of love that transcends self and brings a man to do what is necessary for his fellow Marines even at the risk of his own life, the brotherhood-of-war mentality that only a combat soldier can understand. They were truly a team, and Jim reflected on his good fortune to be their platoon leader. He could think of no higher calling and privilege than to lead these men into combat. Their training was complete. They were ready for whatever awaited them on an undisclosed island in the Western Pacific.

4

Movement to the Objective

If you know your enemy and know yourself, you need
not fear the result of a hundred battles.
—Sun Tzu, *The Art of War*

In late January 1945, Jim and some 2,000 men of the 3rd Battalion boarded
the USS *Sibley* and began the voyage that would eventually take them to
Iwo Jima. After leaving their camp on Maui, they made a stop at Pearl Harbor for three days where they enjoyed a last liberty. The ship lay anchored
offshore, tethered to other troop ships so the men could easily go back and
forth between ships and visit some of their buddies in other outfits. Each
company was allowed one day ashore for recreation.

Just before the *Sibley* set sail from Pearl Harbor, Joe Rosenthal, a combat
photographer came aboard ship.

The morning after they left Pearl Harbor, the officers were summoned
to the wardroom. In the middle of the mess table was a plaster model of an
island shaped like a pork chop. A low murmur rose from the officers as they
crowded around the model. Presently Lt. Col. Alexander A. Vandergrift
entered the room. Someone said in a loud voice, "Attention on the deck,"
and all the officers came to attention immediately. Vandergrift walked to
the front of the room and said, "At ease, gentlemen. What you see before
you is a model of the island you have been training for. Its name is Iwo
Jima." He pointed to a wall map of the Pacific behind him and explained
to the gathering of officers the rationale for taking Iwo Jima.

"For those of you who have been in other campaigns, this one will be
different. The Jap general, a guy named Kuribayashi, has planned something different for us this time. According to aerial photographs, he has
buried what we estimate to be the entire 20,000-man garrison *underground*.

All of his defensive positions are also underground. We haven't seen much above ground, but we know they're there. The Navy has been pounding the entire island for weeks, so hopefully a lot of his guns have been knocked out, but I wouldn't count on it.

"Now, I won't belabor the point about how important it is to take this island. We wouldn't be here if the brass back at Pearl didn't think it was necessary. D-Day is scheduled for 19 February. The good news is that the 24th Marines have been assigned to regimental reserve. We aren't scheduled to go in until D+1. The bad news is that, based on what I've seen and heard, we may have to go in sooner. You are now dismissed to meet with your company commanders for more specific discussions."

Jim and Lieutenants Walker and Ware followed Lieutenant Makowski up on deck, where they sat down. Makowski pulled out an enlarged map of the island and pointed to the southeastern shore. "As Colonel Vandergrift said, this side of the island is the preferred landing site. This point here," pointing to the southernmost part of Iwo Jima, "is Mount Suribachi, the highest point on the island. The 5th Division is responsible for the left side of the beachhead next to Suribachi. The 23rd and 25th Marines will be landing to their right on Yellow and Blue beaches, next to an area called the East Boat Basin. The three battalions of the 24th Marines will be waiting offshore for the word to land when and where we are needed to reinforce either of these two beaches as the tactical situation dictates." He spent the next hour explaining their battalion's assignment using aerial photographs.

Just as the three lieutenants thought the briefing was over, Makowski said, "What I've just told you is the plan, assuming we land on the beaches on the east side of the island." Then almost conspiratorially, he went on. "Craig, if we can't land over there, the 1st Platoon has been given a special mission. Now, it may not even be necessary, but you need to be prepared just in case we have to land on the other side of the island. If the weather and the surf are okay, then we land on the east beaches, the preferred landing site. But if on D-Day they are not suitable for landing, then the plan calls for landing over here." He pointed to the beaches on the west side of the island. "You see this?" He indicated a small island about 2,000 yards off the northern end of the beaches. "It's called Kangoku Rock. Aerial photographs indicate that the Japs have some guns on this island that could give our boys a rough time should we have to land on these beaches. *If* we have to land there, then you and your men and some engineers will row to this island in rubber rafts under cover of darkness—before H-Hour. Once you land, you are to rapidly move inland and secure it as a tentative site for an artillery battalion that will provide support for the beach landings to follow. You will remain there and give the engineers close support in order to protect them from close-in enemy counterattack."

Jim was thrilled by the prospect of leading his own little invasion. Secretly, he hoped for it.

———•———

The straight-line distance between Pearl Harbor and the Marianas by way of the Marshall Islands was about 4,000 miles, but naval vessels in time of war did not travel in a straight line. Because of the threat from Japanese submarines, they traveled in a zigzag pattern. The constantly changing directions of the ships made them less vulnerable to torpedo attacks. This extra precaution more than doubled the distance they had to cover and therefore the time it took to reach the staging area in the Marianas.

The USS *Sibley* was designed for transporting troops, not for their comfort and entertainment. The accoutrements and arms of war for an entire battalion seemed to fill every nook and cranny.

Life on board ship was boring. Except for a few other ships of the armada that stretched to the horizon in both directions, there was nothing to see except the boundless expanse of the Pacific Ocean. The officers were keen to keep the men occupied. There was little room for physical exercise, so the best that could be done was to engage in regular, in-place calisthenics. It was not ideal, but it was better than nothing.

The Navy provided one source of entertainment. One of their aircraft carriers was not far away, and several of its Corsair planes flew patrols near the *Sibley*. Jim stood on the deck to watch as they practiced low-level attack runs. They flew so low that when they passed the *Sibley* they appeared to be skimming over the water.

Jim took advantage of the free time to review the operational plans with his men. He showed them photographs that indicated the location of Japanese pillboxes and machine gun positions in the area just inland from the beaches where they were to land. He showed them detailed maps of the island that pinpointed the locations of known Japanese positions. They reviewed the maps and photos until they had them memorized. He also went over the contingency plan for taking Kangoku Rock. At the very least, this exercise kept the men busy.[1]

Many of the men spent their free time writing letters to parents or girlfriends or reading. When one guy finished a book, he would pass it around to the others to read. After chow one day, Jim and some of his men wandered up to the deck to enjoy the cool of the evening. The usual conversation soon fell to a serious discussion about a best-selling novel they had been reading. One of them asked, "Hey, Lieutenant, have you read this book?" He handed Jim a dog-eared copy of *The Robe*, by Lloyd C. Douglas.

"No, I haven't. What's so special about it?"

"You gotta read it, sir. Several of us have read it, and afterwards, well, we've got no fear anymore. We're not afraid of dying. We're ready to do what we have to, no matter what happens."

Jim was touched by this sentiment and their solicitude. What was it about this particular book that so moved them? It was not until after the battle that he found out. *The Robe* is the story of Marcellus, a Roman soldier, who wins Christ's robe as a gambling prize at the Crucifixion. He then sets out on a quest to learn the truth about the robe—a quest that reaches to the very heart of Christianity. It is a timeless story of adventure, faith, and romance, a tale of spiritual longing and ultimate redemption. In the end Marcellus is sentenced to death for treason. He walks bravely to his death without regret, knowing that God is with him. When Jim finished reading it, he understood exactly what his men had been talking about that cool evening on board the troop transport. The story had prepared them for whatever fate awaited them. They had been ready to face the possibility of death on Iwo Jima without fear.

Jim's platoon had two guys who had some previous boxing experience. A makeshift boxing ring was built on deck, and each platoon offered its champion for several bouts. Card games were also popular. The men particularly enjoyed pinochle and cribbage. Jim was quite the pinochle shark. In his experience, the best way to win was to bid whether he had a winning hand or not. He often bid himself into a deep hole, but as long as he was bidding, his opponents were prevented from scoring points. To the consternation of his men, Jim often won using this unorthodox strategy.

He spent some time with his men in desultory conversation. These times of jocularity served to further cement the close relationship developing between Jim and the men of the 1st Platoon. During the day when he reviewed the plans for the invasion with them and ran them through calisthenics he was Lt. Craig, their platoon leader. During the evening the lieutenant bars, figuratively speaking, came off and he was just one of the guys, sharing good times together. For some, it would be the last bit of fun they would enjoy in this life, but for the moment they could put aside thoughts and cares of the looming battle and enjoy a bit of fun at cards and banter.

Before "lights out," he and some of his men engaged in what came to be known as "bull sessions." They would talk about their families, their girlfriends—and associated conquests. Sometimes they became philosophical. Sometimes they wondered what would happen once they hit the beaches.

Some of the veterans in Jim's platoon had seen action on Saipan and Tinian in the Marianas. During one memorable bull session, they recounted a grisly story about the fate of some of the Japanese civilians on Saipan. Toward the end of the battle the Marines had pushed the Japanese back into a pocket near some high cliffs. Thousands of Japanese men, women, and children had holed up in caves in the cliffs. Marine interpreters urged the civilians to surrender. Unfortunately, the Japanese government had told the civilians that they could expect no mercy from Americans. They believed this propaganda and chose to die rather than surrender. Whole families wrapped a sash around themselves and together jumped over the side of the cliff to be dashed on the rocks below, to drown, or to be killed by sharks. Hundreds if not thousands committed suicide, despite pleas from the Marines that they would be treated well. When the Marines searched the caves, they found children with their throats cut. Parents had murdered their own children rather than surrender them to the Americans.

This story had a profound effect on the men of the 1st Platoon because it demonstrated the fanatical mentality of the people they were about to attack.

Bushido—The Way of the Warrior

It is a common misconception that the fanatical mentality of the Japanese soldier came from the *bushido* philosophy. *Bushido* is an ancient Japanese martial code of conduct. In its original understanding, it was an honorable code teaching righteousness, courage, humanity, propriety, sincerity, honor, and loyalty. Following the first Sino-Japanese War of 1894–95, however, Gen. Yamagata Aritomo ordered that all Japanese soldiers must commit suicide rather than surrender to the enemy. This marked the beginning of the modern Japanese corruption of *bushido*. This corruption of *bushido* permeated the Japanese military elite during the first half of the twentieth century and was part of the training and indoctrination of ordinary Japanese soldiers. Therefore, the fanatical mentality demonstrated by Japanese soldiers in World War II did not originate from *bushido* but from a corruption of it.

Source: Yuki Tanaka, *Hidden Horrors, Japanese War Crimes in World War II*

Throughout the long voyage to Iwo Jima, the photographer Joe Rosenthal climbed all over the ship to get the best angles for photographs of the men studying charts and maps or engaged in calisthenics. He was one of several combat photographers assigned to cover the Iwo Jima operation, but it was his picture of the six men of the 28th Marines raising the flag on Mount Suribachi on D+4 that catapulted him to fame and earned him a Pulitzer Prize.

An otherwise shy man, Joe took an interest in how the men spent their free time. One evening he began watching a game of cribbage Jim was playing with another Marine. He asked him how the game was played, and Jim was only too happy to explain it to him. Soon Joe and Jim were playing four-handed cribbage with a pair of Marines.

One job that Jim performed was Officer of the Day. The OOD checked on the various sentry posts scattered around the ship to make sure they were manned and that the sentry was alert. It took him about two hours to make the rounds. This was not particularly bothersome during the day, but making the rounds at night, under blackout conditions, could be dangerous, as the ship was completely dark. On occasion Jim stumbled across the dark deck over myriad cables and other obstacles. It took so long to make the rounds under these conditions that no sooner had he completed the first round than he had to start the next. Fortunately, because there were eight other junior officers, he had to pull this duty only once every nine days.

Early in February they spent three days at Eniwetok in the Marshall Islands, taking on fuel and waiting for the other ships of the armada to catch up. His men were not allowed to leave ship, but the OOD went ashore to get the mail.

They continued on to the Marianas and dropped anchor off the beautiful island of Saipan. The next day they began the final leg of their voyage, which would take them to their deadly date with destiny.

5

Welcome to Hell

War loves to seek its victims in the young.
—Sophocles

In the early dawn of 19 February 1945, the 485-ship armada carrying the Fifth Amphibious Corps (VAC)—more than 70,000 Marines from the 3rd, 4th, and 5th Divisions—arrived off the coast of Iwo Jima. The planners could not have picked a better day for the invasion. The weather was ideal with a seven-knot breeze, a few scattered clouds, and relatively calm seas so that the invasion boats could land on the preferred east beaches. Jim had been notified earlier that the alternate plan to land on the west side of the island, in which his platoon was to seize the little island of Kangoku Rock, was not necessary. He and his men would land with the rest of the battalion.

Jim and Ed Cavalini woke up around 4:00 AM after a fitful sleep to the booming sound of the big naval guns shelling the island. Since the 24th Marines were held in regimental reserve, Jim did not have to do anything special that morning. He and Ed had their usual breakfast of scrambled eggs and bacon in the officers' mess.

They then went up on deck to watch the unfolding invasion preparations. Jim was greeted by a cacophony of deafening blasts as the big guns fired salvo after salvo at the island. It was still dark, so the yellow blasts from the naval guns silhouetted the ships of the armada and the island against the horizon in a momentary, ghostlike spectacle. He was mesmerized by this otherworldly tableau.

As the sun rose, the outline of the island gradually became more distinct. Jim's first impression was that it was an ugly island, especially after the beauty of Hawaii. He found the shelling and explosions somehow reassuring as he watched smoke rise from hundreds of exploding rounds on the beaches. It was an impressive display of naval might. Surely, he thought, nobody on the island could possibly survive such a brutal pounding. He went so far as to speculate that the Navy would end up doing the job for him and that this would be a short campaign with few casualties.

At 0630 Vice Adm. Richmond Kelly Turner gave the order to land, raising the curtain on the bloodiest and most famous campaign in Marine Corps history. Jim watched in awe as wave upon wave of landing craft bearing the invasion force churned through the water to the beaches just behind the rolling barrage of naval gunfire. Following the bombardment, carrier-based planes flew in low, strafing the beaches with machine guns and rockets. When the planes had cleared the skies, the Navy opened fire again with another punishing bombardment to further soften up the beaches just as the landing craft were approaching.

Iwo Jima Beach Defenses

Responsibility for the defense of Iwo Jima was given to Lt. Gen. Tadamichi Kuribayashi, a 53-year-old combat veteran of the Manchurian campaign. He had been handpicked by Emperor Hirohito himself. This assignment carried a heavy burden, for Kuribayashi knew that if Iwo Jima fell to the Americans, the Japanese Home Islands would inevitably fall. He therefore pledged to the emperor that he would defend Iwo Jima to the death.

Early in the war, Japanese commanders had tried to defeat landings on the beaches as Marines poured ashore, when they were most vulnerable. In every case, they failed. The Japanese defenders had been cut down like a scythe by overwhelming naval gunfire. So in May 1944, Col. Naoyuki Kuzumi, charged with the defense of the island of Biak northwest of New Guinea, chose not to defend the beaches against MacArthur's soldiers. Instead, he conceded the beaches from the outset and holed up in cave-poked hills and gorges, there to chew up the soldiers in a battle of attrition. As a result, the island held out for three months and Japanese generals on Saipan and Peleliu resolved to follow the colonel's example. In each case, the Marine Corps still defeated the Japanese, but at a tremendous cost in casualties. Based on this experience, Kuribayashi chose to defend Iwo Jima in the same way.[1] Since he could not stop the Marines, he decided to extract from them such a high price in blood that they might think twice about invading the Home Islands. He, too, would fight a battle of attrition.

Kuribayashi also had the benefit of the lessons learned by the Germans who were unable to defeat the American landings on the Normandy beaches the previous year. They, too, had tried to stop the landings at the water's edge and had failed. In previous island campaigns in the South Pacific, the Marines had perfected amphibious tactics and despite enormous casualties had succeeded in taking one island after another in a series of campaigns that brought them ever closer to Japan.

Kuribayashi was determined not to squander his limited resources defending the beaches with suicidal counterattacks. He planned to hold out from heavily fortified static defensive positions for as long as he could. To this end he constructed underground bunkers connected by a network of tunnels throughout the island. Designed by some of Japan's best mining engineers, these tunnels were craftily concealed and capable of withstanding all but a direct hit from a heavy caliber shell. He distributed his men, ammunition, food, and water so that no movement above ground would be necessary once the attack began.

Heavily fortified underground defensive positions covered both the east and west landing beaches and the terraces inland by direct fire. Similarly fortified positions dug into the slopes of Mount Suribachi had a commanding view of the beaches all the way to the East Boat Basin just northeast of beach Blue 2. These positions consisted of artillery pieces and large mortars that could enfilade the landing craft approach lanes offshore, the entire eastern beach, and the terraces inland all the way to the two airfields.

The ground inland from the beaches between the airfields and north of the beaches was heavily fortified and protected by large minefields. These commanding positions provided direct observation of the beaches and preregistered artillery, mortar, and rocket fire over the entire beachhead. Direct fire missions between the beaches and the airfields would continue from these positions until individually captured or destroyed. There was no part of the landing beaches, the steeply sloped terraces, and the flat ground between the airfields that was not covered. Additionally, there was no natural cover to protect the advancing Marines. In the face of horrific fire, they would have to advance over a flat lunar landscape of volcanic ash and rock.

———·—·———

While he stood on the deck, leaning against the rail, Jim listened as reports started coming in over the public address system. The initial waves had landed on the beaches unopposed. Within a short time several thousand Marines were safely ashore. It was eerily quiet. Jim took heart at this news. Maybe this was not going to be so tough after all. He did not know it yet, but the Japanese were so well dug in that the shells had not degraded the defensive positions as hoped.

Kuribayashi's men were well disciplined. They waited until the Marines had made the initial landings and the beaches were packed with men and amphibious tanks before they opened fire with a murderous barrage of their own. Suddenly the beaches erupted with explosions as preregistered mortar rounds and machine gun fire rained down on the Marines. An amphibious landing force is most vulnerable during the initial landing phase, while the attackers are exposed on the beaches. The lightly armed landing troops are confused, possibly sick from the ride in, and there is usually insufficient heavy armor ashore to back them up. This was Kuribayashi's best chance to defeat the invasion and turn back the Marines.

The initial landing forces were caught in the open with nothing for cover. Marines started dying at an appalling rate. Some were cut down with bullets from an unseen enemy, but many were blown apart as mortars landed all around with surprising accuracy.[2] The cry "Corpsmen" could be heard up and down the beach as wounded Marines pleaded for medical assistance.

From these reports, Jim knew they were in trouble. Some outfits had been completely wiped out. The amphibious tanks that had preceded the infantry troops, having trouble maneuvering in the loose sand, were knocked out before they could bring their guns to bear. The beaches were becoming cluttered with wrecked vehicles, dead and wounded Marines, and beached landing craft. It was utter chaos, yet Jim remained confident that the Marines would prevail.

The 23rd and 25th Marines of the 4th Division had landed on the right-hand side of the beaches, Yellow 2 and Blue 1. Jim's regiment, the 24th Marines, with each of its three battalions on its own ship, continued to wait in regimental reserve for the order to land. The 24th Marines were prepared to land on either beach, as the tactical situation required. Bad news from the beaches continued to pour in. Excessive casualties made it necessary for the reserve battalions to land as soon as possible.

At 1405 the order was given for the 1st Battalion (USS *Hendry*) and the 2nd Battalion (USS *Mellette*) to prepare to land on beaches Yellow 1 and Blue 1. After all the landing craft had been successfully loaded and lowered into the water, they rendezvoused just behind the line of departure in front of the troop ships and waited for the order to proceed. With choreographed precision, they maneuvered for the attack. At 1500 they set off, lined abreast in an impressive display of coordination. They left behind a white wake that made it easy to follow them in.

While Jim watched from the deck of the *Sibley*, he heard the announcement, "Now hear this. Now hear this. All troops prepare to disembark." With this announcement his stomach cramped. He thought, "Ooooooh boy, this is it." But within a second the crampy feeling vanished. He did not have time to dwell on what lay ahead; he had a job to do. He gathered his men together and went up on deck to their rail-loaded boat. When they were ready to board, he heard another order over the public address canceling the disembarkation order. He speculated about the reason for the change. Maybe the landings were going so poorly that the beaches were deemed unsafe for them to land. If true, it was a foreboding thought. Based on the initial reports from the beaches, he was somewhat relieved. Maybe he would get to spend another night on board ship.

At 1600 he heard the order again blare from the public address system: "Now hear this. Now hear this. All troops prepare to disembark." This time he did not experience the crampy feeling in his stomach, and he was certain that the order would not be rescinded. He knew he was heading in.

Jim and his platoon boarded two landing craft. Under the command of Sgt. Studs Darnell, half of the 1st Platoon boarded their boat by climbing down the side of the *Sibley* over cargo nets. Darnell and his men got loaded without difficulty, while Jim and the other half of the platoon boarded a rail-loaded boat. A rail-loaded boat was also a Higgins boat, but it was lowered to the water by a crane. Jim and his men did not have to climb down the cargo nets. There were not many rail-loaded boats, and it was considered a luxury to board this way.

Once in the water the coxswain maneuvered away from the *Sibley* and circled while the rest of the battalion loaded their boats. As they waited for the other boats to get ready, the men of the 1st Platoon stood up and looked toward the beach; they were naturally curious. Once they were lined up abreast at the line of departure, everybody was to get below the gunwale[3] for the ride in. When all the landing craft were ready, the coxswains lined them up and waited. The order to proceed was given at 1810, and the first wave of boats began the 4,000-yard run to the beach Blue 2. Five minutes later, the second wave began its run, and then the third, until all were away. The last wave hit the beach at 1855.

Each man in the platoon carried a light pack containing a poncho, shovel, spare socks, a canteen of water, his rifle, four or five hand grenades, and a cartridge belt stuffed with as many extra clips of ammunition as he could carry.

The two landing craft bearing Jim and 41 Marines of the 1st Platoon churned toward the beach. During the 30-minute ride, the shelling continued unabated. On their way in they passed the big battleships and cruisers that were firing at the gun emplacements in the interior of the island. The seas were relatively calm, so the ride was smooth and nobody got seasick. Standing in the back next to the coxswain, Jim stole a glance at the other boats in his wave; they were lined up perfectly. As they rode in beneath the barrage, Jim could hear the whistle of the shells arcing their way to the island. The noise from exploding shells was thunderous. It was unlike anything they had ever experienced before. In a perverse sense, it was thrilling.

No amount of training can adequately prepare a man for his first encounter with combat. He can know his job perfectly and feel confident in his ability to do his duty, but the first time he charges onto a hostile beach where men are dying, he never really knows how he will react. Jim could see the anxiety on the faces of his men, but he did not have time to think about these abstractions. He was not afraid—he did not have time to think about fear—and there was too much on his mind to dwell on the anxieties associated with combat. He had a job to do and a responsibility to his men.

Once they were on the beach, he had to quickly link up with the other half of his platoon and then make contact with the rest of the company. These concerns occupied his mind as they drew closer to the beach. He and his men were as ready as they would ever be. Still, this was his first battle. He did not really know what it was going to be like. He was to find out soon enough. The beaches loomed just ahead.

The scene from the beach was one of exploding shells throwing up dirt and smoke, beached landing craft, wreckage, and hundreds of Marines crawling along the sand. It was as if he were looking into the maw of hell. He ran through his mind one last time what he would do once they hit the beaches. It was imperative that they get out of the boat, up onto the beach below the first terrace, and spread out as quickly as possible.

Suddenly Jim became aware that the boat was slowing and then it drifted to a stop a few hundred yards off the beach. He looked at the coxswain with incredulity. "Why are we stopping?" he yelled.

The coxswain stammered, "Uh, sir, I'm waiting for the rest of the boats to line up." Jim knew they had to get on the beach as soon as possible, that idling off the beach made them sitting ducks for a mortar or artillery attack. It was all Jim could do to keep from punching the hapless sailor. He pointed his rifle directly at the coxswain's chest and said, "No, you're not. You get this son of a bitch on the beach right now." The coxswain did not need any further prodding. He put the engine in gear and proceeded.

As the landing craft neared the beach, Jim took his position at the front of the boat directly behind the landing ramp. The boat suddenly jolted to a stop as it hit the beach. All the men were thrown forward, falling into one another and scattering their guns and grenades in the bottom of the boat. Had it not been such serious business, it would have been a comical scene. After they quickly picked themselves up and reattached grenades to their belts, they tried to lower the ramp, but it would not budge. The sudden stop had jammed it. Stuck in the boat like this put them at great risk. One well placed shell could wipe out half of the platoon before they even got in the fight. Frantically he and his men banged away with their rifle butts until the door finally lowered to the sand. Jim looked to the right at the other landing craft bearing the rest of his platoon. It had landed at precisely the same time as his.

As platoon leader, Jim was the first one out of the boat. As he stepped on the beach he narrowly avoided a severed arm lying in the sand, palm up. The sight of the severed arm was forever seared into Jim's memory as his first image of Iwo Jima.

As his men began to pour onto the beach, Jim yelled, "Keep down and spread out." Mortar rounds and other shells were landing about 100 yards in front of them, one every few seconds, but nothing close—yet. They were below the first terrace, which at least offered a little protection from machine gun fire. As soon as everybody was safely ashore and spread out, he asked, "Is everybody okay?" The squad sergeants reported that everybody was accounted for and okay. Jim told everyone to wait there and keep their heads down until he found out what was going on. He got no argument.

He spotted a man standing next to a tank and recognized him as somebody he had met on Maui. Staying crouched, he ran to him. On his way he passed a shell hole about 6–7 yards across. Plastered around the sides of the hole were the mangled bodies of eight dead Marines. It was obvious that these men, clustered together rather than spread out—as he had ordered his men to do—had taken a direct hit from a mortar shell, which killed them instantly. He slowed down only long enough to take in the grisly sight before moving on. Within the span of only a few minutes, he had been introduced to the horrors of combat. Men were dying, and there was a very real chance that he might be next. He ran up to the man by the tank and asked, "Where's the front line?"

The man replied, "You're standing on it." Jim was shocked. He looked around and saw shells landing everywhere. There were no Marines ahead of him. He was right in the middle of the battlefield. The man said his tank had been knocked out and could not move. As far as he knew, all the tanks that had come in with him had also been knocked out. They had been easy targets because it was so difficult to move them through the loose volcanic sand.

Soon after Jim got back to his men, a runner from the Company CP (command post) arrived and told him he was to move his platoon down the beach and join up with the rest of the company. He looked at his men, who all looked back at him expectantly. These were his men, and he felt the burden of responsibility for them that comes with command. It was twilight, and they needed to move to their new position, dig in for the night, and prepare for the expected counterattack.

He led them up over the first terrace and out into the open again. He did not have to remind them to keep their heads down. He quickly located the rest of the company below the second terrace, where he ordered them to spread out and dig foxholes. Because of the loose sand, their shovels proved ineffective. The sand was so coarse and loose that every time a shell exploded the resulting concussion shook the ground and the holes quickly filled in with shifting sand. They found that their helmets were better for digging foxholes.

As he was digging, Jim's helmet hit something, producing an unmistakable metallic clink. He froze. During the briefings he had been told to expect land mines, and he was certain he had just found one. He marked the spot and backed away as slowly and carefully as he could. He dug another hole several yards away without further incident.

He noticed that the camouflage material had come off his helmet. Now it would make an inviting target for a Japanese sniper. He looked around but could not find the loose material. Then he realized that his poncho was made of the same kind of camouflage. Using his bayonet, he cut a piece out of the poncho large enough to cover his helmet.

When he was finished, his foxhole was large enough to protect him from everything except a direct hit. He got in and peered over the edge to get a lay of the land. He and his platoon were 75–100 yards inland. The flat part of the island with Motoyama Airfield No. 2 was ahead of him about 500 yards away. The terrain in between was pocked with shell holes. Some high cliffs loomed to his right that overlooked the East Boat Basin. To his left about two miles down the beach stood the rounded mountain, Mount Suribachi, the predominant feature of the island and its highest point.

After a while it became eerily quiet again, and Jim began to relax. The calm abruptly ended with the beginning of a series of explosions about 200 yards in front of their position. This was followed several seconds later by a second barrage 100 yards closer. Jim ducked down in his foxhole. This was called a rolling barrage, and the next salvo was going to be close. It landed in front of them, but not close enough to hurt anybody. The next one landed behind them. Shortly after this Japanese barrage began, the Marines answered back with a barrage of their own. The Marines had not had time to bring up their big artillery pieces. All they had were some small caliber mortars (60mm), but this was apparently enough because the shelling stopped after the fourth salvo.

The Japanese had large spigot mortars (320mm), a rocket-assisted, crude, but frightening weapon. Jim had heard the sounds of other mortars and artillery shells, but the noise of the spigot mortar when it went off was the loudest one yet. They nicknamed it the "Screamin' Meamy," and everybody knew when it had been launched because its arc through the air was visible, especially at night. It looked like a skyrocket. Spigot mortars were not particularly accurate, and most landed well out to sea. The frightening part was that he could see and hear it, but he never could be sure where it was going to come down.

Shortly after the Japanese barrage and the Marine answer, Jim received orders over his walkie-talkie from Lieutenant Makowski back at the Company CP to take his men and move forward across Airfield No. 2. He passed the word to his men, and they quickly made their way across the airfield, running around several shell holes along the way. To his surprise, they were not fired upon. When they were across the airfield, they crouched down and spread out. Jim radioed to Makowski that they were in position and awaiting further orders. To his surprise, he was told to return to their original position. Jim did not understand what was going on, but he was not one to question orders. He complied with the order, and they returned to their original position on the beach.

By 2030 the entire battalion was ashore and dug in for the night. The three platoons of L Company had consolidated their positions and established firm contact with the other two companies of the battalion. After the sun had gone down, Jim settled into his foxhole. The Marines expected a large Japanese counterattack. This was their usual practice and something the Marines were prepared for. If the Japanese launched one of their patented banzai attacks, the Marines were ready to mow them down with concentrated machine gun fire and mortars. But Kuribayashi had learned from previous island campaigns that these attacks were nothing more than glorified suicide attacks. There was no banzai attack that night.

———•••———

After 18 hours of some of the most brutal fighting of the Pacific war, with little cost to the enemy, the Marines had suffered 2,312 casualties. It had been a bloody and costly day, but the Marines had put ashore over 30,000 men and were firmly entrenched.

When President Franklin D. Roosevelt was told of the invasion and the initial casualty figures, he shuddered. Jim Bishop wrote, "It was the first time in the war, through good news and bad, that anyone had seen the President gasp in horror."[4]

Despite sporadic shelling during the first night on the beaches, it was relatively quiet, and Jim was able to get a few hours of sleep. The first thing he did each morning was to go around and check on his men. All were accounted for except Private Bachtel. A mortar round had landed close to Bachtel's foxhole, and he had died from his wounds. His body had already been evacuated to the rear. Jim had lost his first man, someone he had known personally. Combat was no longer an abstraction; it had become a very personal reality. He sat down and pulled out a small black book in which he kept a list of his men. He made a notation next to Bachtel's name indicating his platoon's first causality—a KIA (Killed In Action). Sgt. Darnell, a veteran of other campaigns, saw Jim writing and said, "You know, Lieutenant, once you start writing in that little book of yours, you'll never stop." Jim reflected on this for a moment. Bachtel was dead, and there was nothing he could do about it. The finality of death of one of his men was hard to accept at first. He was, however, certain it would not be his last. But he could not dwell on this. He had to get on with the job, which was leading those men who were still alive and able to fight. It seemed coldhearted, but he had to maintain this detached perspective if he was to be an effective leader. It was time to move on.

After he had eaten his breakfast of K rations, he got a call from Makowski, who was about 25 yards further back. "J.C., what was that loud explosion last night?"

Jim did not recall any loud explosions other than the sporadic mortar rounds. "Hold on a minute, sir." He asked Darnell.

"Yeah, a jeep took a direct hit. Didn't you hear it?"

Jim looked over the edge of his foxhole. The mangled remains of a burned-out jeep were no more than 25 yards in front of their position. He asked himself, "How could I have missed that?" He returned to the radio. "Yes, sir. It's right out in front of us. It's a jeep, and it must have been hit by a mortar."

For the next two days the 3rd Battalion remained in its fixed position in reserve while the other two battalions moved out to engage the Japanese. The reserve battalion was supposed to take advantage of this rest period to clean their rifles and otherwise be prepared to move out on a moment's notice.

Under most circumstances, to be in reserve well back of the front meant relative safety, a time to rest and relax. This was not possible on Iwo Jima. The island was so small and the enemy positions of observation were so good that hardly anyplace on the island was considered safe.[5] Those in reserve were still subject to harassment by occasional enemy mortar and artillery rounds. The Japanese had every square yard of the beaches zeroed in with preregistered guns and mortars.

During the second night, a member of Lieutenant Walker's 2nd platoon was killed. His foxhole had taken a direct hit from a mortar round. Jim went over to talk with Walker and saw the foxhole. All that was left was a shoe with a foot and part of a leg still in it. The foxhole was pink and white around the sides with blood and tissue mixed in with the black volcanic sand.

During the first three days ashore, Jim and his men never saw a live Japanese soldier, but during that brief period more than 100 Marines of the 3rd Battalion were either killed or wounded, a casualty rate of roughly 20 percent—and they had not even begun to engage the enemy. Jim had heard from Makowski that the 23rd Marines on the far right flank of the beachhead were suffering so many casualties that Lt. Gen. Clifton B. Cates, the CO of the 4th Division, said of the 23rd Marines, "If I knew the name of the man on the extreme right of the right-hand squad, I'd recommend him for a medal before we go in."[6]

It was very frustrating for the Marines during these three days in reserve. They lost many men to the sporadic shelling and had not yet fired a single shot at the enemy. Natural curiosity got the better of some of the men, who stood up out of their foxholes to see what was going on as if they were tourists. If a large enough group stood together, they attracted the attention of the Japanese, who then lobbed in a few shells. Jim had to constantly remind his restless men to stay down.

During the day they had to remain in their foxholes so that when the order came they would be ready to move out. During the night they continued to receive sporadic artillery and mortar rounds. Except for a little rain on D+2 the weather remained mild. Because Iwo Jima was a volcanic island, the ground beneath them could get quite warm; some foxholes simply became too hot to sit in. The weather did not particularly bother Jim, but he could not say the same for the food.

The usual meal was the often maligned K ration. These rations were packaged in a wax paper box. It included a hard piece of cheese, some bacon, a few crackers, and a piece of hard candy. Iwo Jima had no natural fresh water supply. All the drinking water had to be brought forward from aboard the ships. This water had been brought from Hawaii and was seven weeks old. Jim thought it tasted as bad as any water he had ever drunk. To counteract the terrible taste, he popped his K ration hard candy into his canteen to give the water a little flavor and make it more palatable. During the whole time Jim was on Iwo Jima, he never had enough to eat. At times he was so busy that he did not eat at all, and when he did, the K rations never seemed to be enough.

During the afternoon of D+3 (22 February) Jim received orders from a company runner to be prepared to move out with the rest of L Company under cover of darkness to relieve the 2nd Battalion of the 25th Marines. He passed the word to his men.

A guide from the 25th Marines led L Company 100–150 yards further inland and to the right. To reach the front lines they had to scramble up some cliffs. Once they were in position behind BLT 2/25, he and his men dug in for the night. Because they were much closer to the Japanese positions and because there had been reports of Japanese infiltration attempts during the night, two men shared a foxhole. While one slept, the other stood guard. After a set period they switched.

While his men dug their foxholes, Jim decided he would go a little further forward to see if he could contact anybody. He had not gone far when he heard a voice in the dark say, "Hey, stop, J.C. You're in front of your own lines." Jim did not need any further urging. He quickly scrambled back to his foxhole. In the morning he would enter the fray.

———·——

Front lines was a term used freely by the Marines to describe the relative location of the extent of their forward movement in relation to Japanese-held territory. It probably was a more useful term as applied to the front during World War I when there was an easily defined part of the battlefield, one held by the Allies and one held by the Germans. In between was a so-called no-man's-land. One army's gain in territory was the other army's loss, and one army might make a gain one day only to lose it the next. The front lines were fluid, moving forward or backward depending on the caprice of battle.

On Iwo Jima, because the Japanese hid themselves in a warren of caves interconnected by a system of tunnels that allowed them to move freely from one part of the island to another, there were no defined Japanese lines. Occasionally the Marines simply bypassed a Japanese position. When this happened, that position was then behind the Marine lines, apparently cut off from the main body of the Japanese defenders. But because of the tunnel system the Japanese could move back and take up another position that had not yet been overrun by the Marines. Also, the Japanese in a bypassed position could harass the Marine rear so that at times it seemed the Marines were surrounded, being fired on from every direction.

Depending on who and where you were relative to the shooting and the dying, the definition of the front lines varied. Battalion CP was the furthest back near the beach. They controlled the 81mm mortars, the .50-cal machine guns, flamethrowers, and demolition teams. They considered themselves to be on the front lines, even as far back as 100 yards. Company CP was about 25–50 yards back. They controlled the .30-cal machine gun and 60mm mortar sections, and they considered themselves to be on the front lines. But as far as Jim was concerned, the front lines were as deep as his chest because he was the front line. It was the Marine rifleman who defined the extent of the front line. The front line only moved as far forward as the platoon rifleman. If he had to pull back, then territory was relinquished and the front line moved back with him. When he moved forward, the front line moved lockstep with him.

As the front moved forward, the company CP moved with it, including its 60mm mortars. Positioned a few yards behind the front lines, one 60mm mortar was assigned to cover each of the three platoons. Jim could radio back to the mortar team covering his platoon to fire on one of three relative positions ahead of his part of the front, "1" for the right side, "2" for the center, directly in front, or "3" for the left side. After the initial rounds were fired, he could radio back to correct the aim.

Every night the Japanese tried to infiltrate the lines in front of L Company. They would quietly crawl up to the Marine line of foxholes, foraging for food and water or simply to harass them. When they were able to get close enough to a Marine foxhole, they would toss in a grenade or two. Any activity heard in front of the Marine positions was therefore assumed to be the Japanese and a legitimate target. The Marines had learned from previous campaigns to be ready for it.

The use of passwords is as old a trick as warfare itself. Some Japanese, having been educated in the United States, could speak reasonably good English, but they all had trouble pronouncing English words with the letter L. The Marines knew this and usually picked a password with lots of Ls. The password was changed daily for obvious reasons. One password that Jim remembered as being particularly effective was *lollapalooza*. No Japanese soldier, no matter how good his knowledge of English, could pronounce this word correctly.

A favorite trick the Japanese liked to employ to lure unwary Marines out of their foxholes and into the open was to pretend to be a wounded Marine. This tactic had been used successfully in other island campaigns, but the Marines had learned this lesson and were ready for it. From out in the dark they would hear someone call, "Corpsman" or "Hey, Joe. Somebody come help me. I'm hit. Help me." The Marines did not fall for this trick. Anything like this brought an immediate and violent response from the Marines. A flare was fired, and then the front lines erupted in rifle and machine gun fire.

The Marines communicated in some cases by way of landline telephones. Another trick the Japanese used at night was to find the line and follow it back to a foxhole and toss in a few grenades.

During their first night on the front lines, the men of the 1st Platoon heard some noise out in front. Jim ordered a flare shot into the air, which slowly descended by a parachute, illuminating the terrain. Several Japanese soldiers were spotted in the open. All at once everybody started firing. Jim radioed the enemy's relative position to the mortar teams and ordered them to lob a few rounds at them.

Another way to illuminate the terrain at night was with a star shell. When the Marines wanted a wider area illuminated, they notified Battalion CP, who in turn notified the ships standing offshore. The ship responsible for that part of the island fired a star shell that exploded overhead, releasing a brilliant magnesium light that floated down on a parachute. This illuminated a large part of the terrain.

When a Marine confronted a live Japanese grenade in his foxhole, he had only two practical courses of action to take. If he could reach the grenade quickly enough, he might toss it back where it came from. A more natural reaction was to jump out of the foxhole. During the first night on the front lines, a Japanese soldier got close enough to toss a grenade into the foxhole occupied by Dick Crockett and Bill Smith. The grenade landed near Smith, who immediately jumped out. Crockett fumbled for it to toss it away, but before he could, it detonated, killing him instantly. Another notation went into Jim's black book.

———•———

When one company relieved another, the relieving company would come up and dig in directly behind the one to be relieved. The next day, before the scheduled jump-off, the company to be relieved would fall back through the lines as the relieving company moved forward to take its place. In this way the front was never left undefended. This relief did not always go as smoothly as planned because of harassing fire from the Japanese, which occasionally slowed the whole process down.

King-Hour, the hour designated as the jump-off time for beginning the advance, was scheduled for 0730. A 30-minute artillery and naval barrage followed by a 15-minute air strike preceded the King-Hour to further soften up the enemy positions in the zones that the Marines intended to attack.

Because of the rugged terrain, L Company was not able to effect the relief of 2/25 until 0830. By 0850 all units were ordered to move out. Jim received the order by radio from Lieutenant Makowski to get his men up and moving. The objective for the day was the southeast end of Airfield No. 2.

He and his men got up and began to move forward. They had not gone far when they came upon the bodies of the Japanese they had killed during the nighttime firefight. From stories he had heard from other campaigns Jim knew that the Japanese liked to booby-trap their dead with grenades because they knew that Americans were avid souvenir hunters. Several Marines had been killed or maimed in other campaigns while trying to get a battlefield memento off a dead Japanese soldier. Jim ordered his men not to touch the bodies.

They proceeded slowly, looking around for any sign of the enemy. In nearly all cases they did not find the Japanese; the Japanese found them. Unfortunately, the first indication was usually when the Japanese started shooting or when a Marine suddenly went down, shot. The Marines did not waste any time trying to find the source of the shooting but dove for cover behind anything that offered protection. To simply flatten on the ground for very long invited a mortar attack. Unlike the beaches, the terrain further inland was rugged with cliffs and ravines, which offered places to take cover. There were also plenty of shell holes to dive into that offered protection.

Late in the morning Jim received a radio message from Makowski to report back to Company CP. When he arrived, Makowski was uncharacteristically excited as he handed him a pair of binoculars. "Here, take a look at the top of Suribachi." Jim adjusted the lens to bring the top of Suribachi into focus. He could distinctly make out the colors of the American flag fluttering in a stiff breeze. Because of the attendant noise of the ongoing battle, Jim had not heard the cheering or the horns blowing from the off-shore ships when the flag went up. His cribbage partner, Joe Rosenthal, had snapped the soon-to-be-famous picture of the flag being raised.

"Yes, sir. It's a pretty sight. I'll get back to my men and tell them. We've been so busy that we didn't see it go up." As he made his way back, he pondered what the flag represented. He took a pragmatic viewpoint. At least now, he thought, we can forget about that part of the island and concentrate on our part. There would no longer be a need to divide the forces.

Until now the 5th Marine Division had been assigned the task of taking

Mount Suribachi and the southern part of the island. With Suribachi in Marine hands, all effort could be directed at the center where the 4th Division was slugging it out against the most heavily defended part of the island. The 5th Division turned its attention to the left flank of the front, advancing toward the northern end of the island. Eventually the 3rd Division, waiting offshore in floating reserve, was inserted into the lines between the 4th and 5th Divisions. The 4th Division pivoted to the right and advanced on the right flank. The three divisions moved more or less abreast across the midsection of the island and began to push northeast against the entrenched Japanese defensive positions.

———•———

Some of Jim's men reported that they had seen a Navy observation plane crash a few hundred yards in front of them. They asked if they could go up and check for survivors. He gave them permission if they took enough men along for protection. An hour later they returned. There were two men in the plane. One had been nearly cut in half by the front seat and was obviously dead. The other was still alive, and they were able to free him from the wreckage and evacuate him to the Battalion aid station, where he received medical care. They did not encounter any enemy fire during their little foray.

———•———

During a lull in the fighting Jim decided to reconnoiter a small ridge just in front of his position. He crawled out of his foxhole and ran to just below the top of the ridge without receiving any fire. He stopped to catch his breath, then slowly raised his head to look over the top. Before he got high enough to see, he thought better of it and ducked back down. He then took off his helmet, stuck it on the end of his rifle barrel, and slowly raised it until his helmet cleared the top of the ridge. Almost immediately a bullet shot through the helmet, putting a perfectly round hole in the front and a blowout hole in the back. As he put his helmet back on, he thought, "Those Nip sons of bitches." He was so mad that he unhooked a grenade from his belt, pulled the pin, and tossed it over the ridge, then darted back to his foxhole. Before he made it back, he heard an explosion, but he was not about to go back to see the results.

When he returned to his foxhole, he radioed the Company CP and requested some grenade launchers. Using these launchers, his men fired several grenades over the ridge near where he had been. The ridge fell silent after this little barrage, and the next day they were able to continue the advance over the ridge.

———•——

At 1500 Jim received orders from Lieutenant Makowski to dig in for the night. They had advanced about 150 yards—a good day. At the end of every day they were ordered to "tie in for the night." Sound military doctrine called for filling gaps in the advancing line between individual units. The front of the advance, rarely very straight, was usually an undulating line with some units out in front of others. Because of varying degrees of encountered enemy resistance or because of the terrain, one company might advance further than the one next to it. This created gaps on the flanks of the unit out in front of the others that the enemy could exploit—flanks were relatively undefended. If a unit got too far out in front, it risked becoming encircled by the enemy. On Iwo Jima a gap presented an avenue through which the Japanese could infiltrate during the night. To prevent or reduce flank gaps, a unit might have to halt an advance if it got too far ahead of the unit to either side of it, or it might have to pull back a little. In some cases another unit might be called up from reserve to fill a gap. To "tie in" meant to consolidate the lines by filling in any gaps.

Jim and his men dug foxholes and prepared the line for possible Japanese infiltration attempts during the night. This time they placed small pipe bombs out in front of their line of foxholes. When a Japanese soldier tried to sneak up on them and ran into one of these pipe bombs, it blew up and alerted the Marines. A flare illuminated the area and the exposed Japanese were shot. Nobody went out to check on them during the night, but the next morning as the Marines jumped off they frequently ran across the bodies of the Japanese they had shot during the night.

Cross Island Defenses—Charlie Dog Ridge

The classic military approach to a static enemy position—flanking and encirclement, coming at a defended position from one or both sides, away from a direct line of fire—was difficult on Iwo Jima because of General Kuribayashi's elaborately constructed and cleverly concealed defenses. In taking some positions, the Marines were able to employ this tactic, but in many others the terrain was not suited for this approach or the position was simply too well protected and defended. Assaults were further hampered by the rugged terrain, which often precluded the use of tanks. The Marines were left to attack as best they could with little else but what they could carry in their hands and on their backs—rifles, grenades, machine guns, satchel charges, and flamethrowers.

Kuribayashi's troops were well disciplined. They usually held their fire until the Marines were within point-blank range, then they fired with machine guns and rifles with deadly accuracy. Many attempts were made by the Marines to take a position before it finally fell to a determined attack and almost always at a high cost in casualties. Kuribayashi had ordered that no Japanese soldier was to surrender but must fight to the death. His proclamation read: "Above all else we shall dedicate ourselves and our entire strength to the defense of this island. We shall grasp bombs, charge the enemy tanks, and destroy them. We shall infiltrate into the midst of the enemy and annihilate them. With every salvo we will, without fail, kill the enemy. Each man will make it his duty to kill ten of the enemy before dying. Until we are destroyed to the last man, we shall harass the enemy by guerrilla tactics." In nearly all cases, the Japanese soldiers dutifully followed this order and defended their positions until they were destroyed and all the defenders killed; very few Japanese were captured during the Iwo Jima campaign. Because the Japanese soldier had no choice but to fight to the death, he fought with a tenacity and ferocity that bewildered the western sensibilities of the Americans.

Taking and securing Airfield No. 2 was a major objective of the 4th Marine Division. The approach to this airfield from the south was dominated by a steep, rocky ridge the Marines named Charlie Dog Ridge. This ran along the southeastern edge of the east-west runway of Airfield No. 2. It got this name from its map coordinates—grid squares 183 C and D. A prolongation of this ridge formed a semicircular rise of ground, a natural amphitheater 70 feet high. From atop this ridge the Japanese gunners and mortarmen had an unobstructed view of the southern approaches to the airfield and used this height advantage with lethal effect. Nearly 100 reinforced concrete bunkers and pillboxes with concealed machine gun, artillery, and mortar positions were buried in three tiers within the sides of the amphitheater. These protected positions could bring to bear concentrated fire from multiple directions. The Japanese could fire from nearly point-blank range at the advancing Marines, who had no warning until fired upon and in some cases had no natural cover.

Land mines impeded tank movement, and antiaircraft guns were used against ground troops. These guns fired shells timed to explode directly overhead with deadly accuracy. Many of the Marines were killed not by bullets but by fiery pieces of shrapnel spewed in all directions by exploding shells.

Gyokusai—Glorious Self-annihilation

Why did the Japanese soldiers defending Iwo Jima fight so fanatically? Why did they not consider the surrender option in the face of such utter hopelessness? An understanding of Imperial Japanese wartime psychology provides the answer. The Japanese garrison at Iwo Jima knew that the Marine landings were imminent. They also knew that they were cut off from any hope of resupply and could expect no reinforcements. They had to know they had no hope of stopping the Marines and were therefore doomed. Because of General Kuribayashi's order, they knew there was to be no surrender and that they had to fight to the bitter end. In the process, they were to inflict as many casualties on the Marines as they could before they themselves were killed.

To contemplate certain death, coupled with the intense mental strain brought about by constant artillery pounding and dwindling supplies of food and water, the Japanese were pushed to the limits of endurance. In his cogent analysis of Japanese war crimes, *Hidden Horrors*, Yuki Tanaka wrote that the intense psychological pressure forced on the Japanese left them with no other choice but glorious self-annihilation. "The idea of gyokusai was to force a Japanese soldier to destroy his most precious possession—his own life, i.e., a person who must face *gyokusai* was forced to recognize how dispensable his life was. For this reason, a soldier had to find his own profound meaning for his death in order to commit the act. He gained a false sense of immortality through his belief that his life would continue through the spirit of the emperor or *kokutai*, 'the national body.' It is ironic that the more desperate the situation Japanese soldiers were in, the more fiercely they fought to show strong loyalty toward the emperor so that their spirit might live on." The closer the Marines got to the Home Islands, the more desperate the situation became for the Japanese defenders and the more fiercely they fought.

Ordinarily, and certainly in all other occasions except combat, when an enlisted man comes into the presence of an officer, he jumps to attention and salutes him. Because Japanese snipers tended to single out Marine officers as high-priority targets, everything was done to make the officers indistinguishable from the enlisted men. They were never to be saluted, and one did not come to attention in their presence. Another trick to divert attention from officers was to make them appear like the enlisted men. All Marines wore the same uniform and did not otherwise wear anything that called attention to their rank. Jim did not wear lieutenant's bars on his lapels. The only way to identify him as an officer was by an emblem on the back of his dungaree jacket. The emblem identified his unit as it did for all Marines, both officers and enlisted men. A code number on the emblem indicated his rank, but it was too small to be seen by the enemy.

As soon as he hit the beach on D-Day, Jim ditched the carbine that the officers carried and picked up an M1 rifle. By the time he landed, there were several available from dead and wounded Marines. In addition to making him look less like an officer, the M1 was also a better weapon. In all outward appearance he was just another grunt and therefore no more of a target than any private. In fact, he thought he was the most private-looking officer on the entire island.

Jim's preference for the M1 over the standard carbine was based on its superior stopping power. In his experience a bullet fired from a carbine did not always bring a man down. Unless it was a head shot or some other vital part, the man might continue his attack until he was hit again. A shot from an M1 usually brought the man down regardless of where he was hit. Its stopping power was a function not of the bullet caliber—they both fired .30-cal.—but of its higher muzzle velocity relative to that of the carbine.

All Marines must eventually come to grips with the possibility that they might be killed. They develop coping mechanisms to deal with this possibility. One way was simply to deny one's own mortality; it was always going to be the other guy who got killed. It did not take long on Iwo Jima for Jim to develop a way of coping. At the end of the day, he was alive; that is all that mattered. And then the next day, he was still alive. From one day to the next, then from one hour to the next, he was still alive. He kept condensing the time frame to smaller intervals until it was down to the second. Right now, at this moment, he thought, "I'm still alive and okay." In this way he was able to carry on without cracking.[7]

Jim envisioned three possible outcomes: (1) He would be killed outright and probably not even know it. Death would be instantaneous with no pain, in which case he would not have to face the hell of combat anymore. (2) He would be wounded and evacuated, depending on the seriousness of the wound. (3) He would survive with only a minor wound or without a scratch and walk off the island when it was all over.

There was intermittent small arms fire during the night, and L Company reported some enemy infiltration in front of its line, but most of the enemy were killed. At 0915, following the preparatory artillery barrage, the attack began with the three platoons of L Company moving out together toward the high ground.

Jim's primary job as leader of 1st Platoon was to lead his men as they advanced toward the day's objective. At first they advanced slowly and cautiously, ready to dive for cover the moment the Japanese started shooting. They seldom saw a Japanese soldier shoot at them.

As they advanced across the rugged terrain, they suddenly came under an intense mortar barrage. They all hit the deck and crawled to the nearest cover. Jim and five of his men dove into a large shell hole while mortar shells landed all around them. The noise was deafening as one round after another pounded into their position. Fortunately, the soft volcanic ash attenuated the round's blast effect. Still, the concussion was tremendous. The Marines instinctively covered their helmets and ducked their heads as sand and dirt rained down on them from close hits. The sound of deadly shrapnel zinging overhead was unmistakable. Anybody unfortunate enough to be caught in the open was killed immediately or he received mutilating wounds. If one of these shells landed next to a Marine, he might simply disintegrate in the blast. Later, bits and pieces of human flesh and bone and the odd piece of uniform or boot might be found, but sometimes nothing was left by which the body could be identified for burial. In some cases the coffin of a dead Marine shipped home to the family was empty—there was simply nothing left to send home.

The barrage was so intense that Jim was forced to concede the ground, and he yelled to his men that they were pulling back. The mortar fire would have to be silenced one way or another before they could move forward. The best way to get his men safely out was to order them back in pairs between salvos. After the next salvo landed, he turned to the two nearest men in the hole with him and yelled, "Go." When they were safely away he waited for the next salvo. When it landed, he immediately pointed to the next two and yelled, "Go." They jumped out of the shell hole and started to run. They had gone only about ten feet when the next salvo landed near them. Jim and the remaining Marine huddled in the shell hole and waited for the next salvo and then they, too, got up to run back. As he ran from the hole he nearly stepped on what was left of the body of one of the two men who had left before he had. Its head, left arm, and the entire left side of its torso had been blown off; they were simply gone. Blood and shreds of tissue were scattered all around.

For the most part Jim was able to maintain a detached, stoic attitude over the loss of his men. Naturally, it grieved him to lose any of his men, but he had to keep his emotions in check for the sake of the men still in the fight. If they saw their platoon leader start to lose it, they, too, would be adversely affected. On the surface he might appear to be cold and callous toward the death of one of his men, but he had to be. The rest of the platoon depended on him to keep his cool. He was their leader, and one of the best ways to lead is by example. Even with the obscene mutilation of the Marine's body, Jim had to put aside his emotions and revulsion and carry on with what had to be done. The battle did not allow him time to mourn. He still had a job to do that required his full attention.

The horrible way in which the Marine had died shocked Jim. He leaned up against the side of rock and sat there, unmoving. His men noticed that he appeared to be in a daze. Sergeant Darnell, concerned by this uncharacteristic behavior, radioed the situation back to Company CP. After a minute or two, Jim seemed to snap out of his catatonia. Darnell noticed this and radioed back, "He's okay now." Jim got up and yelled over to Darnell to have some stretcher bearers brought up to collect the body.

The second Marine lay on the ground with blood oozing from his back. Miraculously, he had survived the blast. It had blown him about ten yards from Jim's shell hole, and shrapnel had peppered his back, but he was still alive. One man dragged him back to the shell hole. After another salvo landed, they got out and quickly carried him back to safety. A stretcher was brought up, and the wounded Marine was taken back to Battalion where he received medical care. He survived his wounds and was soon evacuated to the offshore hospital ship where he received definitive care. Later, another stretcher was sent up to the front to retrieve the dead Marine's body.

The Marines took care of their own. Every effort was made to get the dead and wounded off the front lines as soon as possible, even at the risk to others. With rare exceptions they never left a wounded man for more than a few hours. It was part of the Marine psyche. They simply would not leave one of their own out on the battlefield to fend for himself.

It is stating the obvious, but in war two belligerent sides try to kill each other. During the day, men can usually see what they are shooting at, but at night they become a little more nervous and trigger-happy. Matters are made worse by fatigue, a malignant environment, and a natural fear attendant to the darkness. Previous combat experience in the Pacific campaigns by the Marines suggested that it was better to yield the night to the Japanese. It simplified matters greatly. Anyone outside the perimeter, or front lines, was considered to be the enemy and was shot. In yielding the night to the Japanese, the Marines did not give up great tactical advantage. Despite their training, the Japanese could not smoothly coordinate large night assaults. It was no easy matter for them to get close to the Marine lines without raising an alarm by some improvised trip wire or other noise makers. At night the Marines stayed in their foxholes. Any noise out front was assumed to be the enemy and usually brought an immediate response.[8]

One night on the front lines, a Marine from the 2nd Platoon, which was tied in next to the 1st Platoon, must have gotten spooked. He ran directly in front of the 1st Platoon. Jim and his men heard him running, assumed it was the Japanese, and started shooting in the direction of the noise. The next morning, as they started their advance, they found the body of a Marine directly in front of their line of foxholes. They realized it was the man they had shot during the night. In this case, the most likely explanation was that he left his foxhole to go to the bathroom, became disoriented in the dark, and inadvertently ventured in front of the Marine lines. Unit morale was terribly affected by "friendly fire" casualties.

Such casualties are inevitable. Sometimes Marines were killed purely by accident. They were mistaken for the enemy, or the wrong coordinates were given to the artillery. More likely, unknown to his comrades, the unlucky Marine was in the wrong place at the wrong time.

Such was the case one day for Jim and the 1st Platoon. He was talking with Lieutenant Makowski at the Company CP, which at the time was about thirty yards back from where the platoon was dug in. Without any warning, incoming artillery and mortar rounds started landing all around them. Jim instinctively dove for cover next to a rock. It did not take long for the Marines to distinguish the sounds of their own artillery and mortars from the Japanese rounds. Jim immediately recognized that these rounds were coming from his own artillery. The way that the Marines alerted their own artillery that they were firing on friendly troops was to fire a flare in the air. Jim saw "Smokey Bear" fumbling to attach a flare to the launcher of his rifle. Jim was just about to get up and run back to help when "Smokey Bear" finally fired it into the sky, trailing white smoke. The message got through. The barrage lifted.

Soon Jim received a radio message that his men needed stretchers right away; they had taken some casualties. Jim grabbed a couple of stretchers and ran. He saw two of the wounded walking, but the other two were injured severely enough that they needed to be carried back to the battalion aid station on stretchers. He sat down and sighed. Four more men lost to his dwindling platoon.

6

Into the Meat Grinder

For some men . . . the fear of death might be palliated by
the belief that nothing more dreadful could possibly happen
to them than had already happened.
—Marcellus to his slave, Demetrius, in *The Robe*

The pivotal point of Kuribayashi's island defense centered around Hill 382 and the bowl-shaped ridge called the amphitheater. Hill 382 (so named for its height) was located about 250 yards east of Airfield No. 2 and directly north of the amphitheater. Atop Hill 382 stood a two-story reinforced concrete blockhouse with artillery and antitank weapons. This stronghold was surrounded by camouflaged machine gun nests and spider traps. A spider trap was the name given by the Marines to a singular Japanese defensive position. It was a one-man foxhole with a camouflaged steel cover. The soldier hiding in a spider trap would wait until a Marine passed him, spring out, shoot, and then duck back inside.

Each position covered other positions with interlocking fields of crossfire. The caves and network of tunnels beneath the hill allowed the Japanese to reinforce threatened positions or escape when overrun without exposing themselves to fire. Light and medium tanks were dug in turret-deep in the maze of ravines and ridges around the hill with their cannons covering every approach to the hill.

Beneath Hill 382 was a communications center with concrete walls four feet thick and a reinforced roof that could withstand heavy naval bombardment.

Located 600 yards south of Hill 382 was an outcropping of volcanic rock that the Marines named Turkey Knob. It was defended by machine gun nests and mortar pits connected by a network of tunnels.

Minami, located just east of Turkey Knob, was one of five villages on Iwo Jima. Sulfur mine workers who lived in Minami had been evacuated long before the battle. Minami was reduced to rubble by the initial naval and aerial bombardment, but hidden within six concrete buildings was a concentration of machine guns, mortar pits, and sniper-infested spider traps. The surrounding landscape was a jumble of torn scrub trees and sharp rock formations, ideally suited for defense but difficult to attack.

The Marines referred to Hill 382, Turkey Knob, the amphitheater, and the village of Minami as the "Meat Grinder."

———

Each morning a preparatory mortar and artillery barrage preceded the day's advance. Hundreds of shells were fired into the hillsides and ridges at suspected Japanese positions. As soon as the barrage was lifted, Jim ordered his men out of their foxholes and they began to move forward.

Jim looked over the ugly features of the high ground as his platoon approached, trying to get an idea of where the Japanese might be hiding. The features of the amphitheater were apparent, but he could not see any Japanese gun emplacements; they were too well hidden.

At times, the Japanese waited until the Marines had advanced beyond their positions so that they could fire on them from behind or into their flanks. All the Japanese positions had a height advantage over the advancing Marines, so they could toss grenades and shoot down at them. It was next to impossible to take out such a position by a frontal assault without sustaining an unacceptable number of casualties. When confronted by this type of obstacle, the Marines had to fall back to a defiladed position and wait for another platoon to either come around to it from the side or work around to the rear of the Japanese position. If he thought he did not have enough firepower on hand, Jim could call for additional heavy weapons to be brought forward to assist him.

In many cases an enemy position was identified only after a Marine was shot. The advance was then stopped and the wounded or dead Marine was evacuated. Once an enemy position was identified, Jim got on the radio and requested additional firepower. Sometimes he asked for a flamethrower squad if he thought it could get close enough to the cave or bunker entrance without unnecessarily exposing the squad to enemy fire. Other times he asked for "Smokey Bear" to send up a .30-cal machine gun squad. These squads were on-call for his use when needed.

One of "Smokey Bear's" machine gun squads consisted of one man to operate the gun and two men to load it. The second loader was not necessary, but if one man were killed or wounded, the second loader kept the gun operating. All members of the squad were knowledgeable in the use of the weapon. One of the two loaders also carried the ammunition, which consisted of belts that held 250 rounds each. Ideally there would be several belts available. Once they were in position and ready to fire, they were under Jim's operational command.

When the squad arrived, Jim would point out the Japanese position that had them pinned down. The machine gunners would set up their weapons and fire just above the platoon to keep the Japanese inside the caves pinned down while Jim's men or another platoon off to the side and out of sight moved into position. Once they were in position they could toss in grenades or a satchel charge to blow it up and seal the entrance.

A flamethrower was another very effective weapon often used by the Marines on Iwo Jima to eliminate a Japanese position. It killed in two ways. Anybody unfortunate enough to be in the way was immediately inciner-ated. The fire burned up all the oxygen in the cave and suffocated those deeper inside who had survived the flames.

One day the 1st Platoon came under fire from a cave about 50 yards in front of them. One of his men went down, shot through the chest. Jim sent two of his men to drag the wounded man to safety while he radioed back to Battalion for some stretcher bearers. Although badly wounded, the man was still alive when the stretcher bearers evacuated him.

Jim called for a flamethrower squad. When they arrived, he pointed out the enemy cave. While his men supplied suppressing fire to keep the Japanese pinned down, the flamethrower team slowly worked its way around to the side of the cave and got into position. The flamethrowers usually worked in pairs. The man with the flamethrower needed both of his hands to operate it, therefore he could not carry a rifle. He relied on another Marine to protect him as he moved into position. When he was in position near the cave entrance he aimed the flamethrower nozzle inside and let loose with a stream of burning gasoline. They then hurried back. On this occasion, before they could get back to the safety of their squad, the Japanese shot their own flamethrower back out at them. The Japanese flamethrower was not nearly as powerful as the Marine flamethrower, and it did no harm. But now nobody wanted to go near the cave. Jim's men laid down more suppressing fire on the cave entrance while another Ma-rine worked his way above it. When he was in position, he tossed a satchel charge inside.[1] He hit the deck, and a few seconds later a loud explosion erupted from the cave entrance. When the smoke and dust cleared, Jim peered at the cave through his binoculars. The cave appeared to be gone. He and his men cautiously approached, but it was obvious that the cave was completely sealed and that anybody inside was either dead or entombed to suffocate or he had escaped through a connecting tunnel.

With the Japanese position destroyed, Jim's platoon continued the advance. This certainly was not the most efficient way to subdue the enemy, but on Iwo Jima it was usually the only way. The Japanese refused to come out into the open. Kuribayashi was proving to be a shrewd tactician. Although he was slowly losing the battle of Iwo Jima, the Marines were paying a heavy price for it.

On the few occasions when Jim and his men came upon a Japanese soldier in the open, they all fired on him together. Rarely did Jim see a Japanese soldier, put him in his gun sights, and fire on him. On one occasion he saw a Japanese soldier 300–400 yards in front and got off a quick shot, only to miss him. He saw the round strike the dirt next to him, but before he fired another shot, the soldier ran away. Once he was standing in conversation with Lieutenant Makowski when he saw a Japanese soldier running in the distance. He quickly aimed and fired, but missed. Another time he and his men spotted a lone Japanese soldier sitting in a chair in a cave entrance, apparently asleep. They approached without alerting him, and several fired, killing him. Since they had all fired at once, any one or all of them may have hit him. This was not a contest; they were not keeping score, carving notches in the rifle stocks to tally their kills. When they saw a Japanese soldier, they all fired. It did not matter who killed him, only that he was killed. The only score that mattered was, "I'm alive and he's dead." It was that simple.

War is a dirty business, and there can only be one winner. On Iwo Jima the loser nearly always was killed. The Japanese fought to the death, and they did not take prisoners. It is a simple maxim of mortal combat: *You kill the enemy before he kills you.* In mortal combat, by definition, there could only be one of two possible outcomes: kill or be killed. There was no noble concept of fair play in this kind of fight, no Queensberry Rules of combat. That Victorian notion vanished after World War I. The war against Japan was one of annihilation, where the rules of nineteenth-century warfare did not apply. Jim had no qualms about putting an unsuspecting Japanese soldier in his cross hairs and pulling the trigger. Japanese snipers had certainly killed many of his buddies in the same way. On Iwo Jima, it was a fight to the death. Give no quarter and expect none.

One day as they were advancing into the "Meat Grinder," Jim's platoon got held up because of harassing fire from another cave above them. While they awaited reinforcements, a tank pulled up behind them. For the rifleman, the presence of a tank was sometimes reassuring because of its great firepower, but more often than not, it was something that gave him cause for anxiety. A tank could bring to bear a large caliber cannon or flamethrower on an enemy position, and it offered some protection to the riflemen who could advance behind its protective armor. But tanks were also prime targets for mortar and artillery fire.

A telephone located at the rear of the tank allowed somebody outside to communicate with the tank driver inside. Jim ran to the phone to tell the tank commander the tactical situation and where he wanted the tank to go. While he stood there, he felt completely exposed, as if all the Japanese on the island had him personally in their gun sights. He yelled into the receiver, "This is Lieutenant Craig."

"What's going on?" came the reply.

"There's a Jap machine gun position just around the corner on the right. It's in a cave on the ridge about 30 feet up. You can't see it from here, but if you move forward and swing around to the right, you'll be able to get a shot at it."

"Hold on while I take a look." The tank moved forward with Jim walking behind it, the phone still in his hand. As soon as the tank made the turn, a mortar round landed right in front of it. The tank came to a sudden halt and then began backing up.

Jim got back on the line. "What are you backing up for? You're almost there."

"Sorry, Mac. It's way too hot up there." The line went dead.

Exasperated, Jim hung up and moved with the tank until he was out of the line of fire. The tank turned around and left. Jim was almost glad to see it leave. At least it would not draw any more mortar fire. Maybe the tank driver was right. Maybe it was too dangerous out there for the tank. It would not do him any good if the tank got knocked out. They would just have to take out the machine gun position by outflanking it. It was more time-consuming, but he did not have any other choice.

In some cases they were able to simply go around an enemy position. This usually required the coordinated effort of other platoons to keep the Japanese pinned down with concentrated machine gun and mortar fire while Jim and his platoon moved around and away from the position.

In most cases a Japanese position—usually a cave—had a limited field of fire, and if the Marines could move away from its fire lane, they could get around it. This was not always as simple as it sounds because the Japanese had so positioned individual caves and bunkers that they provided mutual fire support. This tactical approach required patience as Marines with heavy machine guns, flamethrowers, and satchel charges slowly and painstakingly moved into position. It was Jim's job to assess the tactical situation and call back to the Company CP to tell them what assets he needed.

Using this slow, laborious approach, one enemy position after another was assiduously attacked and eliminated, allowing the Marines to advance a little further inland. In the process Marines exposed themselves to unseen enemy positions. Many of Jim's men were killed or wounded, not so much in attacking an enemy position but in finding one.

During the assault in the "Meat Grinder," Lieutenants Walker (2nd Platoon) and Ware (3rd Platoon) were wounded and evacuated. Jim did not know their status, but he was acutely aware that of nine platoon leaders in the entire 3rd Battalion who had landed on D-Day, all second lieutenants, he was the only one left. The other eight had been killed or wounded and evacuated. He was the last combat-effective lieutenant in the battalion, and that was a sobering thought. The Marines were losing junior officers so quickly that once when he reported back to the Battalion CP, some of the more senior officers remarked to him, "Hey, what the hell are you doing here? You're supposed to be dead or wounded. Everybody else is."

Because of the high attrition rate among officers, battlefield "promotions" were common. It was not unusual to have a first lieutenant become a company commander, a position ordinarily held by a captain (Makowski, commander of L Company, was a first lieutenant) or a sergeant or corporal (both noncommissioned officers) moved up to the position of platoon leader. They assumed the new position of higher rank, but it was not an official advancement or promotion in rank. When a position was vacated by the loss of an officer, the most able person available filled it regardless of rank. As an example, Jim had to relinquish Sergeant Darnell from 1st Platoon to replace Lieutenant Walker of the 2nd Platoon. On Iwo Jima, advancement and promotion, usually by way of merit and service time, were frequently the result of attrition.

Additionally, when a platoon suffered so many casualties that it essentially ceased to function as a unit, it was broken up and incorporated into other platoons. With the loss of Walker and Ware and many of their men, what was left of the 3rd Platoon was distributed to the other two platoons of the company. Darnell took half of the battered 3rd Platoon, and Jim took the other half.

One of the men that Jim picked up from the 3rd Platoon was Pete Durnan, a sandy-haired, freckled-faced farm boy from Pennsylvania with big dimples. Jim came to like Pete and thought that he was one of the best Marines he had ever met. As soon as Pete was assigned to the 1st Platoon, he made himself known to Jim and said he was not afraid and that he was willing do whatever Jim asked of him. Right away Jim saw leadership qualities in Pete, but he had not been in the Marines long enough for this quality to be noticed, so he was still a PFC.

The fourth day after Pete had been assigned to Jim's platoon, they were advancing into the thick of the defenses around Turkey Knob. High ground on both sides and in front confronted their advance. There was an area about 20 yards across that they had to run through. One by one Jim's men ran forward, zigzagging through the fire lane with bullets flying all around. Eventually one of his men was hit and went down. Jim called a halt to the advance so they could get their man out. They did not know if he had been killed or wounded. Before somebody ran out into the open to pull him to safety, a smoke grenade was tossed in the vicinity to obscure the Japanese line of fire. Jim was about to do this when Pete ran to him and volunteered. Jim, who could see that Pete was eager to do his part, relented.

"All right, Pete, but move fast and stay low. When you get to him, don't waste time. Just drag him back here as quick as you can."

Pete took the grenade and asked, "Where do you want me to toss it?"

Jim put one arm around Pete's shoulder and pointed with the other to the spot. Suddenly a shot rang out that Jim knew was close. Instinctively he hit the deck, but Pete did not. Jim looked up and was surprised that Pete was still standing. The reason was immediately obvious. He had been shot through the back of the head and a stream of bright red blood was pulsating out of the exit wound in the center of his forehead. As Jim looked up Pete slowly slumped to the ground beside him. Blood continued to pump out of his destroyed forehead for what Jim thought was an interminable time. He hated to lose any of his men, but Pete's death was particularly hard. Four years later Jim and Pat named their second son, Peter, in memory of Pete Durnan.

Jim sat there with Pete's body for a few moments, then gently laid him down against a rock out of the line of fire. Unfortunately, in combat one does not have time or the safety to mourn the dead. There would be time for that later. Until then, Jim still had a job to do. And he still had a man down who might be alive and in need of immediate medical attention. He got up and took the smoke grenade from Pete's hand. Then he ran into the open and threw it near the wounded man. When the smoke had obscured the area, two Marines dashed out to him, grabbed him from behind the shoulders, and dragged him back around the rock to safety. The man was alive with only a shoulder wound. Stretcher bearers came up from the beach area and took him back to the Battalion aid station.

Jim was lucky. With only one exception, his platoon never lost a man who had been wounded and evacuated.

———————

Jim's platoon had been advancing through a rocky ravine when they came under a fusillade of machine gun fire. They instinctively dove for the nearest cover. Jim, who had found protection in a shell hole, stole quick glances to see if he could spot the location of the machine gun fire. He saw several places where a machine gun nest might be hidden, but he could not be sure. He spotted a low area behind some rocks off to the right that would provide adequate defilade from the machine gun fire, but to get to it he and his men would have to run through the line of fire.

His men waited anxiously nearby, and when it was quiet Jim yelled, "Go." Each man in turn ran as fast as he could, kept low, and zigzagged all the way until he reached the defiladed position. Jim knew full well that each time he yelled, "Go," he was possibly sending a man to his death, but there was no other way. He was the platoon leader, and it was his responsibility to lead, and one of the responsibilities of a leader during combat is to send men into harm's way.

In a very real sense the outcome of the entire war hinged on the sum of the outcomes of individual battles fought by Marine riflemen. A Marine with a rifle trying to take some ground went up against a Japanese soldier with a rifle trying to defend the same ground.

It was not Jim's job to win the battle of Iwo Jima. It was not even his job to take Charlie Dog Ridge or capture Turkey Knob. Politicians and others of higher rank could plan grand strategies for winning the war and move large armies and navies around on a world map; his job was narrower in focus. It was to lead his men into battle and take out individual enemy positions and thereby move closer to capturing and securing a small piece of real estate. It was "For want of a nail . . ." in reverse.[2] In this case, instead of the war being lost for want of a nail, the war is eventually won by first winning small battles at the platoon and squad levels, which in turn lead to capturing ever larger pieces of territory until finally the entire island is secure. Take enough islands and the war is won. But it starts with the individual Marine and his rifle (the nail in the analogy) attacking an enemy position. All across Iwo Jima, similar pitched battles were being fought as one enemy position after another fell to the Marines. Brave young men put duty above self and did what was necessary to win the objective.

Jim was now confronted with such a battle. There was no way around it. They had to take out the enemy machine gun position. And to do so his men had to run forward to get into better position, which meant running through the gun sites of a Japanese soldier with his finger on a trigger and wanting nothing more than to kill as many Marines as he could before his position inevitably fell.

One by one they ran through the open as bullets kicked up dirt at their feet. When half his men had made it across to the other side, Jim took his turn and darted out into the open. He did not draw any fire. Perhaps the Japanese gunner was reloading, or maybe it was because Jim was simply quicker. This was a situation in which his relatively small stature and quickness was to his advantage. He ran fast, kept low, and zigzagged, changing directions frequently to present to the Japanese as difficult a target to hit as he could. He made it across unscathed. When he reached his men, he motioned for the rest to follow. The last man to go was a guy called Pops Lorenzen. At the age of 31, Pops got his nickname from being one of the oldest ones among the enlisted men. Because of his age he had originally been assigned as a cook. When the need for replacements on the front lines became acute, even the cook was called up. Pops, having spent much of the battle well behind the lines, may not have been as fit as the front line Marines. As he ran across the open, a rifle bullet caught him full in the chest, knocking him to the ground where he lay motionless.

Jim looked on in anguish. He motioned to the man next to him, one of his corporals, to follow. They darted back out into the open, grabbed Pops by the arms, and dragged him back to safety. The corporal knew first aid and took over. He instructed Jim to cradle Pops's head while he tore open his shirt. In the center of his chest was a gaping hole over his heart out of which bright red blood pulsated. It was clearly a mortal wound. As Jim looked on, Pops slowly started to arch his back in a last, rigorous spasm pressing his head down into Jim's cradling hands. Almost pleadingly, Jim looked at the corporal, who just shook his head and said, "Sorry, sir. There's nothing I can do for him." Jim did not want Pops to die on the battlefield, so he called for a stretcher to be brought up. Pops was taken back to the Battalion aid station, where he died.

———•——

Most of the replacements who were added to Jim's platoon were green and relatively untrained, so much so that Jim almost wished he had not gotten any. He needed men to replace those whom he had lost, but some were so inexperienced that, in his estimation, he was better off without them. Some eventually proved their worth and fit in, but not all. He got one replacement, a private named McCarthy, who was from the East Coast. Jim quickly realized that McCarthy did not really know what he was doing. He seemed to wander around the battlefield without a care. Somehow he did not recognize that he was putting not only himself but also others in danger by his actions. Finally Jim had had enough. He grabbed McCarthy by the shirtsleeve, pulled him over to a rock, sat him down, and said, "Stay right there. Don't you move until I come and get you, 'cause you're gonna get yourself killed and maybe somebody else."

"But, sir—"

"Stay put. No arguments."

"Yes, sir."

An hour or so later Jim looked up to survey the battlefield and noticed a dead Marine lying on the ground and asked, "Hey, who's that?"

"It's that new guy, McCarthy, sir."

Jim just sat down on the ground, leaned up against a rock, and tipped his helmet back. What a waste. It was so unnecessary. If McCarthy had stayed put, he might still be alive. Jim was at a loss to explain McCarthy's careless behavior on the battlefield.

His men were getting killed despite his best efforts. Some died because they did not do what he told them, and some died even when they did exactly what he told them. Where was the logic to it? It made no sense. Jim was coming to a stark realization. Events on the battlefield did not always unfold according to a set of rules. Even the most highly skilled, courageous Marine with the best training and most advanced weapons was as likely to get killed as the most reckless and careless Marine was. Life or death in combat was as much a function of luck as it was of training and courage. The randomness of death on the battlefield had become all too apparent to Jim when Pete Durnan, standing next to him, was killed and he was spared.

———··———

As a platoon leader, Jim had two main responsibilities. The first was the success of the mission, and the second was the welfare of his men. Without the latter he could not achieve the former. They were codependent, but the mission came first. Jim recognized that McCarthy's behavior was a risk to the platoon and therefore the mission, but there was little he could do short of ordering him back to the beach. In the end McCarthy got himself killed and there was not much Jim could do to prevent it. He could not be a babysitter for one man; he was responsible to the entire platoon. Jim took good care of his men. He struck a balance between doing whatever was necessary to achieve the success of the mission without needlessly exposing his men to danger.

One of Jim's men, Private Wright, was trying to brew some coffee, a rare luxury on the front lines. He did this by first taking out the liner of his helmet, turning it over, and heating water in it over a little gas burner.[3] This could only be done during the day, since a fire at night attracted the enemy's attention. Before he was finished Jim was called away for about an hour. Unknown to Private Wright, a Japanese flamethrower squad was hidden in a cave near the place he had picked to make coffee. They apparently stuck their flamethrower nozzle out and doused Wright with it. When Jim returned an hour later, he could hardly recognize Wright's body.

———··———

Late one afternoon Jim sent a squad on a reconnaissance patrol. Private Bigler was on the point (out in front) when there was a loud report from a Japanese gun. Bigler immediately toppled over. The rest of the men hit the deck and quickly crawled for the nearest cover. Somebody called out to Bigler, but there was no reply. They retreated to their original position, told Jim what had happened, and asked if they could go back with a stretcher to retrieve Bigler's body.

When they returned, one of them tossed a smoke grenade and white smoke bellowed up obscuring the area around Bigler's inert body. Two men dashed out into the open and pulled him back. He had a large gaping hole in the lower part of his abdomen. One of the men felt for a pulse; there was none. It was only a token effort because it was clear that he was already dead. From the look of the wound, it was obvious that a large caliber round had hit his abdomen and passed directly through, exiting his body without exploding. He quickly bled to death; he never had a chance.

———··———

One evening the Japanese lobbed several phosphorus grenades into positions occupied by the platoons of L Company. Studs Darnell was the 1st Platoon's sergeant who had replaced Lieutenant Walker of the 2nd Platoon. One of the phosphorous grenades went off near Studs, and some of the burning phosphorous got on his forearm and hand. There was no way to put it out. It just kept burning and was extremely painful, but he did not cry out.

———··———

It was relatively quiet on the front one night with only sporadic enemy shelling. The Marines responded with about 300 rounds of 81mm mortar fire. This kind of enemy harassment and Marine response was becoming almost routine.

The next morning word was passed to Jim from the L Company CP that he was to hold his position for the day. They were to reorganize and strengthen their lines by 1200. Throughout the day they continued to receive sporadic harassing mortar fire. Two air strikes and naval gunfire were called in, in addition to regimental artillery fire, which eventually silenced most of the enemy mortars.

At 0500 the next morning Jim was informed that the 3rd Battalion was to be relieved and returned to the rear. A rest was well overdue, Jim thought, as he trudged back to the beach area. On the way back he passed Lieutenant Davis heading in the opposite direction. During some of the company briefings, they had become acquaintances. They stopped briefly and exchanged a few words. Later that same day Jim learned that Davis had been killed. The 3rd Battalion had lost another junior officer.

When Jim and his platoon arrived at the beach, they spent much of the rest of the morning filling sandbags, which they used to build individual little bunkers that would protect them from almost everything but a direct hit. It was a laborious process. Jim was stripped to the waist and sweating profusely. When he was finished digging his bunker, he looked forward to changing into clean underwear and socks. He was wearing the same clothes he had worn when he hit the beach two weeks earlier. There was no need to change his dungaree jacket and trousers; they were still usable, but a change of socks and a clean pair of underwear would be very welcome.

Just as he finished filling the last of the sandbags for his bunker, a runner came to him and said he was wanted back at battalion CP. He put his shirt and jacket back on, grabbed his rifle, and trotted back to the CP, where he presented himself to Capt. Joseph McCarthy, 2nd Battalion, 24th Marines. Jim had become acquainted with McCarthy during the many briefings he had received over the past two weeks.

McCarthy said, "Craig, I know you and your men have been up on the lines without much rest, but there's a gap between the 3rd and the 4th Divisions and I want you to go back up and fill it."

"Sir?"

"You're the only rifle platoon leader left in the 3rd Battalion, and we need to fill the gap." Because of the gains made the previous day, a gap had opened up between the right flank of the 3rd Division and the left flank of the 4th Division. On Iwo Jima the Japanese used these gaps to infiltrate the Marine lines at night. In many cases infiltration attempts were not as much for search-and-destroy missions as they were for foraging for food and water. The Japanese had quickly dwindling supplies, not the least of which was water, which they could not replenish.

"Yes, sir."

"I'll take you up and show you where to take your men. Now, you needn't worry. It's not hot where we're going."

Dodging bullets as they ran through fire lanes, the two men made their way to the front. They stopped behind a little ridge overlooking a low area with another ridge further ahead. McCarthy pointed to the far ridge and said, "I want you and your men to dig in in front of that ridge."

Jim saw the characteristic green smoke of Japanese mortar shells billowing up just beyond the low area. "You're right, sir. This ain't hot," Jim said facetiously.

"Hot or not, we need you here."

"I understand, sir," Jim said, somewhat chastened. Jim liked Captain McCarthy and had a lot of respect for him. There were times when he wished Capt. McCarthy had been his company commander. For his actions on Iwo Jima, Capt. Joseph McCarthy was awarded the Medal of Honor.

As Jim surveyed the area, he noticed a machine gun squad setting up on a hillock off to his right. As he watched, one of the Marines stuck his head up and was immediately shot through the neck by a sniper's bullet. It was a mortal wound, and nothing could be done for him. Jim watched as the Marine quickly and quietly bled to death.

———·—·———

Death came suddenly, without any warning, for many Marines. Complacency and carelessness on the battlefield were usually fatal mistakes. The Marines were constantly aware that danger surrounded them. There was no place on the island that was out of reach of Japanese mortars, and because of the extensive tunnel system, snipers could be anywhere. In this case the Marine was preoccupied with setting up his machine gun and raised his head too high. A Japanese sniper was watching from a cave, waiting for such a tempting target to present itself. One made mistakes of this kind only once. Survival on Iwo Jima required constant vigilance. A Marine could not guard against every mortar shell or bullet, but neither did he put himself at risk by unnecessarily exposing himself to enemy fire. With bullets and mortar shells coming from all directions, every Marine was at risk. But the wary Marine did what he could to reduce the risk by staying down.

Fig. 1. Jim Craig (*back row, center*) with members of Sigma Chi fraternity, Purdue University, 1942. (Jim Craig)

Fig. 2. Pvt. Jim Craig standing at ease outside his barrack at Parris Island, 1944. (Jim Craig)

Fig. 3. Jim demonstrating the textbook-perfect prone firing position with an M1 rifle, Parris Island. (Jim Craig)

Fig. 4. Jim (*front row, far left*) with his fellow boots, Parris Island. (Jim Craig)

Fig. 5. Jim with his parents, Syd and Kathryn, 1944. (Jim Craig)

Fig. 6. Jim and Pat enjoy a moment together in Pat's home in Knightstown, Indiana, 1944. (Jim Craig)

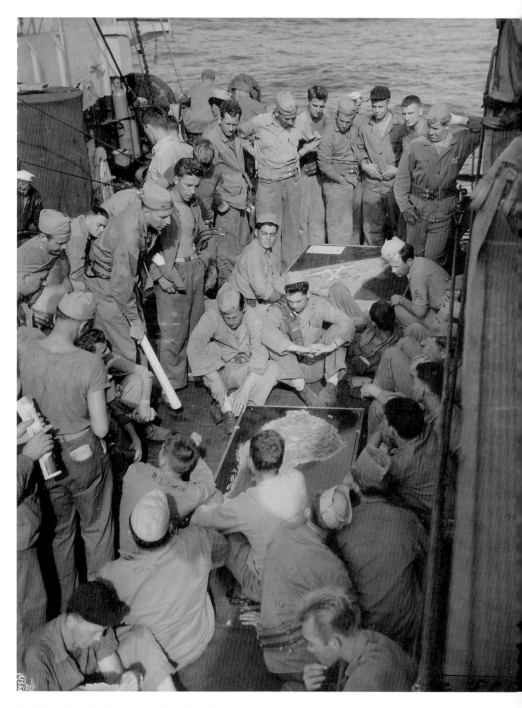

Fig. 7. One day after departing Pearl Harbor, the men were informed of their destination, shown plaster maps of Iwo Jima, and given a briefing by their commanding officers. (Marine Corps University Archives Dept., Quantico)

Fig. 8. When they were not engaged in mission briefings or calisthenics, the men often passed the time playing pinochle and cribbage. (Marine Corps University Archives Dept., Quantico)

Fig. 9. Mount Suribachi today. The white memorial, marking the spot where the flag was raised, is just discernible on the summit. (John Shively)

Fig. 10. Looking down the eastern side of the island from the plateau along the entire 3,500-yard length of the landing beaches to Mount Suribachi. (John Shively)

Fig. 11. Marines board a landing craft on D-Day in preparation for the invasion. (National Archives)

Fig. 12. Several landing craft approach the beaches in an attack wave. (National Archives)

Fig. 13. Waves of Marine landing craft approach the beaches. Beaches Blue 1 and 2 are located on the far right. (National Archives)

Fig. 14. A landing craft, each carrying half a platoon, heads for the beaches. (Marine Corps University Archives Dept., Quantico)

Fig. 15. A landing craft has hit the beach, the ramp has dropped, and the Marines are moving ashore. (Marine Corps University Archives Dept., Quantico)

Fig. 16. Marines cautiously crawl up the first terrace while others hunker down in their foxholes on D-Day. (Marine Corps University Archives Dept., Quantico)

Fig. 17. A Marine takes a cautious peek over the first terrace to get the lay of the land. Mount Suribachi can be seen in the distance. Note the coarse black sand. (Marine Corps University Archives Dept., Quantico)

Fig. 18. Marines take what little cover they can find while enemy mortar and artillery shells rain down on the congested beaches. (Marine Corps University Archives Dept., Quantico)

Fig. 19. Even in death, this young 4th Division Marine seems to be defending his position. (Marine Corps University Archives Dept., Quantico)

Fig. 20. During the period of D+1–3, Jim and the men of the first platoon stayed in their foxholes in reserve behind the front lines on the beach awaiting orders to move out on a moment's notice. (Marine Corps University Archives Dept., Quantico)

Fig. 21. *Facing page, top:* Three Marines cautiously move forward. (Marine Corps University Archives Dept., Quantico)

Fig. 22. *Facing page, bottom:* Marines advancing off the beach taking what little cover is available to them. The Marine in the foreground clutches a flamethrower. (Marine Corps University Archives Dept., Quantico)

Fig. 23. *Above:* Marines advance through some blasted shrubs and trees. In many cases the Marines never saw a live Japanese soldier, so carefully were they hidden in caves and bunkers. (Marine Corps University Archives Dept., Quantico)

Fig. 24. Marines at platoon strength prepare to move out with tank support. (Marine Corps University Archives Dept., Quantico)

Fig. 25. A Marine takes cover as a bunker is blasted. (Marine Corps University Archives Dept., Quantico)

Fig. 26. Two Marines take aim from their foxhole. The Marine on the left holds an M1 rifle with fixed bayonet, while the other aims a shotgun. (Marine Corps University Archives Dept., Quantico)

Fig. 27. *Above:* A flamethrower team has worked its way into position. (Marine Corps University Archives Dept., Quantico)

Fig. 28. *Facing page, top:* Once an enemy position was identified, assets were brought forward to destroy it. Here Marines keep the Japanese pinned down while a Marine with a flamethrower works his way close to the cave entrance. (Marine Corps University Archives Dept., Quantico)

Fig. 29. *Facing page, bottom:* Stretcher bearers carry a wounded comrade past a dead Japanese soldier. (Marine Corps University Archives Dept., Quantico)

Fig. 30. A Marine warily inspects a cave after it has been cleared of Japanese soldiers.
(Marine Corps University Archives Dept., Quantico)

Fig. 31. One of Jim's men, Cpl. Robert Kistler, helps a wounded Marine back to the beach area to receive medical attention at the battalion aid station. (Marine Corps University Archives Dept., Quantico)

Fig. 32. *Above:* Raising the American flag on Mount Suribachi. This photo by AP photographer Joe Rosenthal inspired a nation and came to symbolize the U.S. Marine Corps. It was actually the second flag to be raised on D+4. (Marine Corps University Archives Dept., Quantico)

Fig. 33. *Facing page, top:* A burial detail back on the beaches. Each division had its own cemetery. All Marine bodies were later exhumed and laid to rest in a military or hometown cemetery in the United States. (Marine Corps University Archives Dept., Quantico)

Fig. 34. *Facing page, bottom:* Dedication ceremony for the 4th Division cemetery after the battle. (Marine Corps University Archives Dept., Quantico)

Fig. 35. *Above:* A B-29
Boeing Superfortress,
the largest bomber of its
time and the reason the
Marines had to take Iwo
Jima. (James F. Dixson)

Fig. 36. *Left:* Jim back
in Hawaii following the
battle on Iwo Jima.
(Jim Craig)

Another problem was being large. Large Marines were tempting targets. It is a simple fact that a large man is an easier target than a small man and that a big man usually moves slower than a smaller man. Jim, small in stature and very quick on his feet, presented less of a target than bigger, slower men. He knew a Marine named John Dahl, a second lieutenant with Nordic blond hair, who was about 6 feet 4 inches tall. Paired up alphabetically, they had shared foxholes together at Camp Lejeune. Jim liked John and always thought he would go far in life, maybe even aspire to political office from his home state of Wisconsin. However, John was shot and killed because, Jim thought, he was simply too big and therefore presented an easy target.

Jim went back for his men and brought them up to the front without incident and had them spread out and dig in between the 3rd and 4th Divisions, consolidating the lines and effectively eliminating the gap.

They remained on the front lines between the two divisions for three days until they were ordered to rejoin the rest of their company on D+17. When he was reassigned to L Company, he was disappointed to find that they had not moved any further forward from where he had left them. It had been a hot spot before, and he was eager for them to move on.

Jim and his men were held up because of a fierce firefight to their right one afternoon. When the fighting died down, he went over to see how it had gone. He found the remnants of the platoon that had been engaged in the fight gathered together behind a big rock. They looked cowed and hesitant. Jim had seen this look before. He asked, "Where's Lieutenant Fansler?"

One of the privates said, "He got shot, sir. He's dead and has already been moved back to the beach."

The loss of yet another officer, he thought. His immediate concern was for the shaken men of Fansler's platoon. They were leaderless and scared. They had also lost their sergeants; they were just a bunch of privates and corporals. Usually in this kind of situation somebody naturally steps up and assumes a leadership role. He searched the faces and recognized somebody he thought could fill the void until a more permanent leader could take over the platoon. He pointed to him and said, "You, Marine, on your feet. Come with me." They walked away from the rest of the men, then stopped. Jim turned to him and asked, "What's your name?"

"Corporal McKinney, sir."

"How old are you, McKinney?"

"Nineteen, sir."

"All right, McKinney, your buddies are pretty shook up. I knew Lieutenant Fansler. He was a good man and a hell of a Marine. But he's gone, and those guys need somebody to take command and lead them through this."

"Yes, sir," he said somewhat diffidently.

"Now I know you can do this. When we get back, I'm going to tell them that you're in charge and that they're to follow your orders. They're just looking for somebody to lead them, that's all, and I think you're that man. They'll follow if you lead. You're a Marine. You can do it."

"Yes, sir," he said with a little more conviction.

Jim could see a change in McKinney already. He stood more erect, and his bearing took on a more confident look. He'll do okay, Jim thought. "You ready?"

"Yes, sir. Thank you, sir," he said smartly.

"Let's go."

They moved back to the rest of the platoon. "All right, you guys, now listen up. I'm sorry about Lieutenant Fansler, but he's gone and you guys still have a job to do. Corporal McKinney here is going to take over for now. You are to pay him the same respect you gave Lieutenant Fansler. He's going to be in command until you get somebody else to take over the platoon. You are to follow his orders. You understand?"

There was a collective nodding of heads.

"Okay, McKinney, take over."

As Jim headed back to his platoon, he knew that McKinney was going to do all right. All across the island, platoons like McKinney's were going through the same thing. Junior officers were getting killed or wounded, and somebody had to take over for them. Leaders developed quickly on Iwo Jima.

———··———

The Japanese had a small, handheld mortar that the Marines called a "knee mortar" because it was small enough to launch from the knee.[4] On his way back to the platoon after talking to McKinney, Jim heard the all too familiar sound of one of these knee mortars heading his way. He looked up but did not see it coming until it landed in front of him. He braced himself for the inevitable explosion, but it just fizzled a little. It was a dud.

———··———

There seemed to be no end in sight. One day blurred into the next as they attacked and eliminated one enemy position after another. Eliminating one position meant that they were only that much closer to the next. When they could see the caves, they appeared as black eye sockets peering malevolently down on them.

Unaware of the overall grand strategy for defeating the enemy, Jim's war was confined to that part of the battlefield immediately in front of him, the next cave or fortified position bristling with machine guns, mortars, and hidden snipers. For the men of the 1st Platoon, the cave war was a microcosm of the entire operation, if not the entire war. His strategy was simple: take out this cave or that bunker, then move on to the next one, all the while trying to stay alive. They would eliminate one position, then move forward until the next one began firing on them. They would dive for cover and laboriously crawl along the parched, sulfurous ground to flush out the enemy and then repeat the process. It was monotonous and terrifying. He never knew when or where the next shot would come from.

Jim and his men spent most of their time on the front lines advancing into Japanese-held territory, clearing out caves, and attacking enemy positions. There were, however, a few days when they stayed in their foxholes and did not participate in the ongoing battle. It was during these periods of relative inaction and rest that they tried to get caught up on other activities not directly related to the battle. They cleaned their rifles, wrote letters home, and read copies of *Time* and *Newsweek* magazines that were brought in with the mail and then circulated among the men. They discussed the ongoing battle among themselves and compared their personal experiences with what was being reported in the press. They listened to the battle raging around them and wondered how it was going for other outfits. The most important part of these breaks, besides getting much needed rest, was to remain alert and prepared to move out on a moment's notice when called upon.

When they were available, Jim had a Navy corpsman attached to his platoon. The corpsmen, who were considered noncombatants, were constantly exposed to enemy fire. In many cases the Japanese, contrary to the Geneva Convention, which strictly prohibited targeting noncombatants, shot at corpsmen.

The first three corpsmen assigned to Jim's platoon were wounded and evacuated. The fourth one, a likable guy named Curtis Talley, Pharmacist Mate, 3rd Class from New Jersey, had been with him only three days when one of his men was wounded by a mortar round. Talley did not even need to be told to go. He grabbed his bag of first aid equipment and ran out to the wounded man. Jim yelled for his men to provide covering fire. They all began firing at the suspected Japanese position as Talley ran to the man and went to work. The wounded man was bleeding profusely from a shrapnel wound to his leg. It had obviously hit an artery and if the bleeding was not arrested soon, he could bleed to death. There was no time to pull him to safety. Talley quickly applied a temporary tourniquet to the wounded leg and the bleeding eased. He then took the man's rifle and jammed it into the ground and hung an IV bottle of plasma from the stock. As he was about to insert the IV needle into the wounded man's arm, he was suddenly knocked over backwards. A sniper's bullet had hit him squarely in the head, killing him instantly.

Jim, watching helplessly, could only groan in frustration. In the three days since Talley had been assigned to the 1st Platoon, Jim had grown to like him. He sent some of his men out to drag the wounded man and Talley's body back to safety. Afterwards he got on the radio and sent a call back to L Company. "Sir, this is J. C. Talley, our corpsman, just got killed."

"I'm sorry, J.C. That's four for you, isn't it?" replied Lieutenant Makowski.

There was a pause before Jim replied, "Yes, sir." Then he added, "Sir?"
"Yeah."

"Sir, don't send me any more corpsmen. They're getting killed too easily. They're just sitting ducks out there, despite all the covering fire we give them. Just keep them back there. We'll take care of our own wounded and get them back to Battalion."

"That won't be too much of a problem. We don't have many left anyway."

During the course of the battle Jim was called back to talk with Lieutenant Makowski almost daily. One day on his way back to the front he came upon a dead Marine lying on the ground face up. By now he was becoming accustomed to seeing mangled and horribly mutilated bodies. The sight of this Marine's body, however, would forever remain in Jim's memory. This Marine was handsome and muscular, but it was not these features that caught his attention. This Marine's body was conspicuous by its degree of mutilation. All that remained were his head, upper chest, shoulders, and arms. Jim looked around, but there was nothing left. The rest of the body had been blown to bits. He noticed that the Marine wore a ring on his left hand. Jim dearly hoped that his widow would leave the coffin shut when the body was returned home.

There was a path between the front and the beach that was little more than two tire tracks. The path had apparently been used extensively because the tracks had cut deep ruts into the soft ground. During the night the Japanese used the path as a route to infiltrate the Marine lines. Many of them had been caught in the open and cut down the night before. Several Japanese bodies lay along the path. Marine tanks had also used the path as they moved up to the front and had run over several of the bodies.

On the way back along the path to the front lines after the conference with Makowski, Jim suddenly came under fire. He immediately threw himself to the ground in one of the ruts. It provided enough defilade to protect him from the bullets that were flying all around him. Some dry scrub brush grew along the edge of the path. As he lay in the rut Jim could distinctly hear bullets clipping the little brush twigs not more than a few feet from his head. The only way to stay out of the line of fire was to lie in the rut.

As he crawled forward he soon came to the part of the path where the Japanese bodies lay. They had lain all day in the warm sun and some were so badly crushed from the tank treads that their exposed intestines lay like coiled snakes. Others were grossly bloated. A swarm of blue flies buzzed in clusters in their gaping mouths and eyes. The stench was nearly overwhelming, but he had no choice but to crawl by the stinking bodies. He kept crawling as the bullets continued to fly just inches above his head. Bullets made a sound like snapping fingers as they passed. Finally he reached a point where he was only about 20 yards from his foxhole. He waited until there was a lull in the firing, then jumped up and ran as fast as he could and dove into his foxhole.

After he had recovered from his sprint, one of his men reported that Cpl. Richard Kelly had been shot in the groin. The stretcher bearers were preparing him for evacuation. Kelly was still screaming uncontrollably from the pain. Jim felt confident that once Kelly was back at the Battalion aid station under the care of the doctors he stood a good chance of surviving. But he was wrong. Shortly after arriving at the Battalion aid station, Kelly died.

The Marines received mail almost weekly. Included with the letters from home were special copies of *Time*, *Newsweek*, and *Life* magazines. These periodicals did not include any photographs or advertisements, just news. In one issue there was a report on the battle of Iwo Jima. This was the same news that the folks back home were reading. It was obviously already outdated news by a couple of weeks, but Jim was surprised to read the description of how the battle was progressing, the number of casualties reported, and how "bloody" it was. Because his part of the war was restricted to such a small piece of the island, he had very little knowledge about what was going on even 100 yards away. Jim asked some of his men who had seen action in other campaigns about the reports. "Hey, is this true what they're saying about Iwo Jima? You were on Saipan. How does Iwo Jima compare to Saipan?"

"Well, Saipan was much bigger than Iwo Jima. There'd be times when we would advance maybe a couple of miles in one day. I'd say physically it was more exhausting on Saipan than it is here. But we're losing a lot of guys here, so maybe this is right. Maybe it is bloodier here. At least for us it sure seems bloody."

One day Jim and his men were moving back up to the lines and came upon a Marine lying in the lee of some rocks. No one else was around. Jim called for a break, and they stopped to talk to the Marine. They quickly noticed that he was wounded. On closer inspection it was obvious that he had been hit several times, but despite his wounds, he seemed pretty well off.

"Where's your outfit, Marine?" Jim asked.

"They left me here and kept moving."

"Are you hurt bad?"

"Not as bad as it looks."

"What happened?"

"We was movin' up and a bunch of Japs got me. My buddies were able to pull me out of the line of fire to this spot, then some of the guys cleaned out the machine gun nest with grenades. My lieutenant said somebody would be along for me, but that was over an hour ago."

"Where are you hit?"

"I think he got me in the legs and my ass, but it don't seem like they hit any bones or nothin' vital. Mostly flesh wounds, I think."

Jim radioed for some stretcher bearers.

"Hey, any you guys got a cigarette? I'm dying to have a cigarette."

One of Jim's men pulled out a Camel and gave it to him.

"Thanks, fellas."

Jim and his men waited until the stretcher bearers arrived to carry the wounded man back to the beach area.

One day during a cautious advance, a mortar round landed near Jim, but not so close that he was hit. When he recovered from the blast, he reached down to pick up a piece of shrapnel nearby but immediately had to drop it because it was so hot. He never again tried to pick up shrapnel. Another time a round landed nearby, sending a small piece of shrapnel flying into the clip of his rifle less than an inch from his hand. The rifle and his hand were undamaged, but the clip was shattered.

The next time he was not quite so lucky. A piece of shrapnel hit him on the inside of his left ankle. It hurt like hell, but it was not so bad that it kept him from walking. He had a fairly large hole in the skin, but it was not serious. He kept it clean, and it healed without complications.

———·—·——

One of his corporals, Robert Kistler, received a minor wound to his left lower abdomen that was bad enough to need more than just first aid treatment. Jim sent him back to the Battalion aid station. The doctor thought he should be evacuated to the hospital ship. Another Marine had a head wound. He, too, was to be evacuated. The doctor saw that Kistler was able to walk and asked him to help the other Marine walk to the beach where they were taken to the hospital ship. A combat photographer snapped a picture of the two as they made their way back to the beach.

———·—·——

At the end of each day Jim and his men tied in for the night with the other platoons to eliminate any gaps that might have developed during the day's advance. The typical configuration was for Jim's foxhole to be in the center of the line with his men spaced out every five to ten yards on each side. Supplies in wooden crates were brought up from the beach area every evening and placed behind Jim's foxhole. After his men finished digging their foxholes, they came up to Jim's and got whatever supplies they needed, including ammunition, grenades, K-rations, and water. These supplies were to last them through the next day.

Once they were all settled in, he went to each of his men in their foxholes to see how they were doing and to offer them encouragement.

———·—·——

On 10 March, D+19, the two remaining platoons in L Company, battered as they were, were able to advance about 600 yards to within sight of the beach below the cliffs. Japanese resistance was beginning to diminish as, one by one, their positions were reduced and eliminated, so much so that the Marines were able to move relatively unmolested for much of the day. Jim's platoon, which was down to a mere 10 men, including what was left of 2nd Platoon, made steady progress during the day until they came to relatively flat ground that sloped down to some cliffs overlooking the ocean. As they approached, Jim suddenly called for a halt.

He had been on the front lines long enough, had seen the way the enemy operated, and had become sufficiently familiar with their tactics to suspect that something ahead was not quite right. It was only a hunch, but it was based on bitter experience gained from confronting similar situations many times since he had landed on D-Day. And, one could argue, it had kept him alive this long. As he stared ahead he said to no one in particular, "This doesn't look right. It looks too easy, and it's way too quiet. If ever there was a trap, this is it. I'll betcha the Nips are in there just waitin' for us."

He continued to look it over as he called for his radioman. He then put in a call to Lieutenant Makowski. "Sir, we've advanced against little Jap resistance and are now located at map coordinates 185 G. I've got the 2nd Platoon with me, and we've just stopped in front of an area that looks like a trap. I don't think we should proceed until we're sure it's clear."

There was a pause, then Makowski came on the line. "J.C., you've got to advance. We're only a few hundred yards from the beach." It was not lost on Jim that Makowski had said "we" as if he were up there with him. It was, Jim thought to himself, easy for him to order men forward into a position that he did not know anything about, safe as he was back in the rear area.

"Sir, I can't take these guys in there because I'm sure it's a trap. If we go in there, we're gonna get butchered."

Again, another pause before Makowski came back on the line. "Look, I know you've done this before. You can do it."

By now, Jim was getting a little irritated. "Sir, I won't do it. It's suicide. I've already lost most of my men, and I just can't take them in there until I know it's safe. Look, if you'd come up here and see for yourself, you wouldn't send them in either." Jim was engaged in a dangerous game of brinkmanship. He knew he was being insubordinate with his commanding officer and, in essence, was about to disobey his direct order to advance.

One of the benefits of being on the front lines is having a clearer picture of the tactical situation than those further back at L Company CP. Jim was the commander on the spot and knew better than did Makowski what the situation was. Still, he was obliged to carry out Makowski's order even if he did not know the situation as well as Jim did. Jim was confronted by a classic military dilemma. He could obey an order that, in his opinion, was clearly a mistake and risk the possibility that he and his men would be killed in a hopeless gesture. Or he could ignore a direct order from his commanding officer in the belief that in doing so he was saving his men from what he thought was certain death. He had two choices: obey and advance as ordered, or ignore the order.

Jim sat crouched, holding the radio, and looked at his men. They had come this far and had seen more death than anybody had a right to expect of them. He simply could not take them forward until he was sure it was safe. To do so, in his opinion, would be futile with the likely result being the possible annihilation of what little remained of L Company. Makowski would be a commander with nobody to command. Jim almost smiled at the irony of it. He then made up his mind and crossed the Rubicon. "Sir, I can't do it. It's too dangerous. We're digging in for the night."

There was no reply from Makowski, even thought the radio was clearly working. Jim took the silence as tacit agreement with his decision. He dearly hoped so. He had been out of line, and he knew it, but he was convinced that it was the right thing to do. Oddly, Makowski never mentioned this episode to Jim again. It was forgotten.

He looked at his men and could see the relief in their faces. They, too, had a bad feeling about this and were grateful that their platoon leader had stood his ground. They knew he had stuck his neck out for them. There was more than a natural and understandable self-preservation component to Jim's decision. He cared for his men. They had been through a lot together since hitting the beach almost three weeks earlier and had witnessed the horrible deaths of several of their comrades. His devotion and responsibility to the welfare of his men transcended everything else, even allegiance to his commanding officer. It was that sublime esprit de corps that only a Marine can understand and appreciate. Such was the depth of the love Jim had for his men. He felt an obligation to get those still left off the island alive. They were so close, too. If only they could hold on for a few more days. Surely it was almost over.

Earlier, Makowski had sent out a patrol to see how close they could get to the beach. On returning from their reconnoiter, the patrol reported that they had gotten to within 100 yards of the beach, had encountered none of the enemy, and had suffered no casualties. This finding did bode well for the next several days. Maybe it *was* almost over.

The next day L Company had advanced so far that a huge gap had opened in their flanks that had to be filled before night. By 1600 the left flank gap was filled and the line consolidated, but it took until 2200 to fill the right flank.

As Jim settled in his foxhole for the night, he thought to himself, "I'm still alive."

Jim received word that he was wanted back at the L Company CP. By now it was located in one of the captured Japanese caves. When he arrived, he was motioned to the back of the cave and was told he was wanted on the phone. Who could it possibly be?

It was Donald Beaver, a friend from back home in Pendleton, Indiana. Their dads knew each other, and Donald's dad had gotten word to Jim's dad that Jim was on Iwo Jima. Donald was stationed further back on the beach.

Jim said, "Where the hell are you?"

"I'm back at Regimental. Why don't you come back and see me?"

With a chuckle, Jim replied, "Well, Don, we're fighting a war up here. Why don't you come up and see me?"

There was a pause before he answered. "Well, okay. I'll see if I can rustle up a jeep and see you in a little while."

Don never arrived, and Jim forgot about the whole incident until he was back home after the war at his dad's lumberyard and Donald walked in.

Jim looked up in surprise and said, "Don, what happened? Last time I spoke with you, you were going to come up to the front and see me."

"Well, I was, too. Me and a buddy got a jeep and started out, but suddenly somebody started shooting at us. We turned right around and got the hell out of there."

Later, as Jim reflected on his wartime experience, there were other times that he could laugh about. There was a time when he and his men were sitting in their foxholes while the Japanese were lobbing shells to their rear. Sometimes they could see the shells pass directly overhead, while at other times they could only hear them. The Marines lobbed their own shells back at the Japanese. Jim watched his men as they looked up to see the passing shells. It was like watching a tennis match as their heads went from side to side following the arc of the shells.

Another time during a lull in the battle, Jim was reading a letter from Pat. With the muffled noise of exploding shells in the distance, Jim read a line from Pat's letter that said, "I have a feeling you're not in Maui anymore." It was too much. Jim burst out laughing. He took the letter around to his men to read and they, too, started laughing.

Under the circumstances, it did not take much to get a laugh. With so many of his buddies dying every day, living under the constant threat that he might be the next KIA, with the added stress and strain of combat, the Marine found humor in anything he could. What before the war might not seem funny at all now became comic relief during the hell of battle. It was as if they looked for anything to laugh about to break the cycle of stress and grief over dead comrades.

One night some Japanese tried to infiltrate the lines by following a telephone line back to Jim's foxhole. His men heard some noise out in front, so somebody called for a flare. The flare went up and illuminated several Japanese soldiers in the open. The entire platoon began firing at them until the flare went out. After this incident, the rest of the night passed uneventfully.

The next morning as the 1st Platoon began the advance, they came upon the bodies of the Japanese they had gunned down during the night. Most of the bodies looked like all the other Japanese soldiers they had seen during the battle, except for one. He wore an officer's uniform, but the most distinguishing characteristics were his boots and jodhpurs. They were beautiful leather riding boots. Jim had not seen boots quite like these on any of the other Japanese officers, and no Japanese officer wore jodhpurs. This officer was clearly different, but he dismissed it at the time and forgot about it.

Years later Jim came across a story about Lt. Col. Takeichi Nishi, commanding officer of the 26th Tank Regiment. Nishi was a baron and a dashing equestrian who captured a gold medal in the individual jump event on his horse, Uranus, at the 1932 Los Angeles Olympic games. Taking advantage of his fame, Nishi rubbed elbows with the Hollywood elite and brought a gold Packard with a 12-cylinder engine back to Japan. His exploits were gleefully recounted in the world's press, but his death is shrouded in mystery. Some reports suggest that he committed suicide inside one of the many caves on Iwo Jima; others say he was killed during a last ditch banzai charge. Officially, his body was never positively identified. Based on a description in a book Jim read years after the war, he is convinced that the officer wearing the riding boots and jodhpurs was Baron Nishi.

One day Jim's radioman came running to him and said Makowski wanted to talk to him.

"J.C., I've received word that there's a bunch of Japs not too far out in front of your position who are dressed like Marines. I've also heard that some of them even speak English. I want you and your men to go find them and wipe them out."

Jim was immediately skeptical. It did not sound right. He thought to himself: How do those guys back at L Company know about this and how did the Japs get Marine uniforms in the first place? "Sir, I'll check it out."

He gathered his men together and told them the news and what they were supposed to do. He added, "I don't buy this about the Japs posing as Marines. You guys wait right here while I go up and see what's going on." He grabbed his rifle and took off. His men watched as he darted into the open. He immediately came under small arms fire. Diving into shell holes or behind a rock, he safely made his way to a ridge overlooking the suspected "disguised" Japanese position. He got out his binoculars and peered over the ridge. About a hundred yards in front of him he saw a platoon-sized group of men who were dressed in Marine dungarees. He could clearly see that they were not Japanese. He even recognized some of them. When he had satisfied himself that they were not Japanese disguised as Marines, he made his way back to his men. He had to run the same gauntlet of small arms fire, but he made it back without incident. His men were very relieved when he got back because every time he went down they thought he had been hit. He radioed back to L Company and reported that he had seen the suspected "disguised" Japanese and that there was no doubt that they were Marines.

Jim had been in combat for almost four weeks. He was beginning to develop a sense about the battlefield that can only come from experience. This intuition had not only saved the lives of his men just a couple of days earlier but had also kept him from unwittingly killing Marines. He had learned to trust his instincts.

————

Included in official casualty figures is a category labeled "battle fatigue." For some of the men on Iwo Jima, the stress of combat was too much. The sight of so much carnage, the death of comrades, the concussion and thunderous sound of artillery and mortar attacks, and inadequate sleep was more than some could handle.

During a mortar barrage, one of Jim's men saw a mortar round land near a Marine he thought was his best friend and blow him to bits. Overwhelmed by the death of his friend, his mind snapped. He went wild and was only restrained by the combined efforts of four Marines. It was everything they could do to keep him in his foxhole. Because of his uncontrollable behavior, he posed a danger not only to himself but also to the rest of the platoon. As it turned out, the Marine who had been killed was not his best friend after all. His buddies tried to reassure him that his friend was okay, but it made no difference. His mind was gone. Some of the men got him back to Battalion and he was soon evacuated. Jim never found out whether he recovered or not.

This was the only incident that Jim thought was true "battle fatigue." They were all under a lot of stress, tired, and hungry, yet most handled it reasonably well. Jim was convinced that this was in large part due to the training they had received in boot camp.

Early one evening after a particularly good day's advance, Jim called for a short rest. They found a little hilltop that looked safe and sat down and leaned up against some rocks. Bobby Lee, the 1st Platoon's champion boxer, was chatting with a buddy when a shot rang out. He cried out and grabbed his left arm; he had been hit. The rest of the men dove for cover. Jim crawled over to Bobby Lee and inspected his wound. He had a small wound in the middle of his left arm with a little trickle of blood running down from it, but the odd thing about the wound was the bullet that was embedded in it. Jim grabbed it and it came out easily. To his surprise, the bullet was made out of wood. The Nips never cease to amaze me, Jim thought to himself.

"Bobby Lee, you'd better get back to battalion and have somebody take a look at that," Jim said.

"It ain't so bad. Just put a dressing on it and I'll have it looked at tomorrow. You're going to need me tonight," he replied. Such was the devotion of the men of 1st Platoon for one another. Just as they had learned in boot camp: unit first, self second.

It seemed to Jim that Sundays were particularly bad days for the men of 1st Platoon. They seemed to suffer more casualties on Sundays than on the other days of the week. There was no rhyme or reason to explain it; it was just the way things turned out. After the losses on the first three Sundays of the campaign, he actually dreaded the fourth one.

One day Jim's men showed him a grisly sight they had come upon during a reconnaissance patrol. About a dozen Japanese bodies lay outside a cave. Rather than surrender, they had come out of the cave holding hand grenades against their heads. Together they had committed suicide by blowing their heads off. The sight of the grossly mutilated bodies was sickening, but three weeks of combat, as repugnant as it was, had hardened Jim to the sight of death.

———·—

Two days before they were relieved, Jim and his men were advancing toward the beach when a Japanese soldier suddenly emerged from a cave. At first they thought he wanted to surrender, but then they saw that he was holding a hand grenade to his head. One of Jim's men raised his rifle and yelled, "Drop that, you son of a bitch." They gave him ample time to comply, but when it was apparent that he was not going to drop the grenade and surrender, they all raised their rifles and shot him.

The next day they came upon his body. Lieutenant Young, Makowski's executive officer, was in the area, and after conferring with Jim, he walked up to the corpse, pulled out his pistol, and fired a round into its head. Jim and his men were incredulous. He said to Young, "Sir, we shot that Jap yesterday."

Young replied, "I saw his eyes move. He was still alive." Jim and his men just stood there dumbstruck as Young holstered his pistol and walked back to the L Company CP.

The next day while Jim and his men were out on patrol in a mopping-up exercise, two Japanese soldiers walked toward them carrying a white flag. With yesterday's experience still fresh in his mind, Jim gestured with his hands and pantomimed with his rifle for the two to stop and raise their hands. One of his squad sergeants, who had learned a little Japanese, ordered the soldiers to strip down to their shorts to make sure they were not concealing any booby traps. The Marines had learned through bitter experience in earlier island campaigns to mistrust Japanese soldiers who appeared ready to surrender. Some hid live hand grenades in their armpits, and when they were told to raise their arms to surrender, the grenades fell at their feet and detonated. Many an unwary Marine was killed by this deception. When it was obvious to Jim's men that the two were not a threat, they marched them back to the Company CP. As they were about to hand the prisoners over, Young walked up and said, "All right, I'll take charge of these two," and marched off with them himself. Jim was sure he was going to take credit for capturing them.

There were very few Japanese prisoners taken during the campaign, but of those that were, some were used on burial detail to collect their own dead and bury them in a common grave. The Marines had a special Graves

Registration detail specifically assigned to collect, identify, and prepare Marine dead for burial in one of three cemeteries, one for each of the three divisions. The bodies had to be buried as soon as possible for sanitary and hygienic reasons, but every one of the Marines buried on Iwo Jima was eventually exhumed and returned to the United States for proper burial.

That evening as he sat in his foxhole he consulted his black book and took stock of the situation. Including what was left of the 2nd Platoon, now attached to his 1st Platoon, he only had 10 men left of the 41 who had landed with him. This was not a new revelation, but a disquieting thought occurred to him. If the Japanese decided to launch one of their patented counterattacks tonight, his platoon would be in trouble. He pictured in his mind 500 sake-crazed, screaming Japanese charging over the hill and overrunning their position.

One day he ordered a patrol to scout the area to their front while he stayed back in his foxhole to make notes in his little book. While he waited, a member of the Graves Registration came to him and showed him a list of dead Marines and asked if any were his men. He positively identified two men from his platoon on the list who had been killed, one being Private McCarthy. When the Graves Registration detail left, it occurred to Jim that everybody was gone; he was alone. It was eerily quiet, and that is what concerned him. Who was out there? He was greatly relieved when his men returned from the patrol.

The next day Jim received word that some Japanese had been spotted working their way north, retreating from the advancing Marines. Lieutenant Makowski suspected they would launch a counterattack that night. In anticipation of this attack, a 37mm gun was brought forward and set up next to the 1st Platoon's position and made ready. It was well after dark as Jim leaned up against the front of his foxhole and peered into the night. Earlier, he had gone around to check on each of his men to make sure they had everything they needed and to offer words of encouragement. They were ready. They wanted the Japanese to launch a counterattack because, once they were in the open, the Marines could cut them down en masse. All was quiet when suddenly the 37mm started shooting. Somebody must have gotten spooked. There was no counterattack that night. Jim was furious with the 37mm crew. The premature firing must have dissuaded the Japanese from attempting their attack, and a great opportunity may have been lost.

———·•·———

Japanese resistance began to diminish, and it was obvious the battle was nearing its conclusion. The Marines made large advances during the day, so much so that they actually bypassed what few positions the Japanese still controlled. Their primary mission at this stage was mopping-up exercises to clean out what few pockets of enemy resistance remained.

On one of these days Jim and his men passed through a little ravine with a campfire. The fire was still smoldering, and some food and equipment lay scattered. It was obvious that the camp had been occupied recently and abandoned in haste. The Japanese must have heard them coming and decided to run and hide. So quick was the Marine advance that the Japanese did not even have time to put out their fire and gather up their equipment.

———·•·———

The Marines advanced all along the front and were within sight of the rocky cliffs overlooking the ocean. The enemy shelling and infiltration attempts had dropped off significantly over the past week, so the nights were relatively quiet. When the Japanese had been shelling and infiltrating the lines, the Marines were alert and ready at all times, but with the decrease in enemy activity there was a dangerous tendency to relax.

Late one evening Jim was sitting in his foxhole when he looked up and could hardly believe what he saw. Some men in the company to his right had built a campfire. What better target did the Japanese need? Jim got up and ran over to the campfire.

"What the hell do you think you're doing?"

"Sir, we just wanted to make some coffee."

"And you think there isn't a Jap out there lining you up for a mortar attack?"

"Sir, we haven't seen any Japs for a couple of days, and there ain't been no shelling for the last three nights."

"And that means they're all dead, right?"

There was no answer from the chastised Marines.

As Jim kicked dirt on the fire to extinguish it, he growled, "Don't let me see you even so much as light up a cigarette. You got that straight?"

"Yes, sir."

Stupid mistakes and lapses in vigilance got Marines killed, Jim thought to himself as he walked back to his foxhole. They could not let down their guard for one minute, not on Iwo Jima.

On D+26 Jim and his men were relieved. Their part in the battle was finally over. What was left of the 1st Platoon was to be replaced by the U.S. Army. The replacement troops arrived late in the morning and occupied the area near the cliffs. Jim and his men shouldered their gear and trudged back to the beach area. For the first time since they had landed, they walked with the assurance that they were not being lined up for a mortar attack or that a sniper was putting them in his cross hairs.

Jim was greatly relieved that it was over and grateful to be alive, but his elation was tempered when he contemplated the terrible cost the Marines had paid to help secure the island, especially the men of the 1st Platoon. On their way back they passed by Motoyama Airfield No. 2, where he saw a huge B-29 Superfortress sitting on the runway.[5] He thought back to Colonel Vandergrift's initial briefing on board the *Sibley*: "We're losing bombers to Japanese antiaircraft fire and fighters at an unsustainable rate. Iwo Jima has to be neutralized." Well, they had accomplished their mission; they had taken Iwo Jima, but it had been purchased with the blood of some of the finest men he had ever known.

When they arrived at the bivouac area behind the beach, they were issued fresh clothes. He took a cold saltwater bath and then, for the first time in four weeks, he put on clean clothes. A hot shower would have to wait until he was back aboard ship. Once they were in clean clothes Jim had his men fall in for rifle inspection. Even though the fighting was over, they were still Marines, and Jim was still responsible for them.

One of the first things Jim did when he had some free time was to write a letter to Pat, informing her that he was alive and well and would be leaving Iwo Jima the next day.

That night they ate K-rations and slept in a foxhole for the last time on this godforsaken island. The next day they would board the ship that would take them away from this place where many of their comrades lay buried in the sand of the beaches they had assaulted four weeks earlier.

The next morning there was no preparatory artillery barrage to start the day. It was blissfully quiet. Jim and his men gathered their gear and marched down to the water's edge. A Landing Ship, Tank (LST), its bow doors open for vehicles to drive into its interior, sat partway up on the beach. They walked up a gangway and that was it. They were leaving Iwo Jima.

Unfortunately, the sulfurous smell they had come to know so well while living on the island was now replaced by the eye-stinging, pungent smell of diesel fumes from the many vehicles accumulating in the hold of the LST. Several hours passed before the LST finally backed off and pulled alongside the attack transport that would take them back to Hawaii. Carrying all their gear in backpacks, they transferred to the APA by crawling up cargo nets.

The original plan was for them to lay over in Saipan, where they were to prepare for the invasion of Okinawa scheduled for 1 April, just two weeks later.[6] Instead, they returned to Camp Maui in Hawaii for an extensive rehabilitation period. The 3rd Battalion, one of three in the 24th Marines, had filled an entire ship when it came to Iwo Jima. Because of the large number of casualties, there was room on the same size ship going back for what was left of two entire regiments, the equivalent of six battalions.

As soon as he was assigned a bunk in the officers' quarters, Jim took the most refreshing shower of his life. He washed off four weeks of dirt and the detritus of war. Afterward, he felt like a new man; he had forgotten what it was like to be clean. That evening he ate dinner with the rest of the officers in the wardroom, sitting at a table with a linen tablecloth and silverware and served by a ship's steward. The contrast with the battlefield was almost too hard to believe. His first meal aboard ship consisted of meat and potatoes and gravy. It tasted great, but fifteen minutes after he had eaten, he had to rush to the head where he promptly threw it all back up. His stomach was so unaccustomed to hot food after four weeks of cold, bland K-rations that his body rejected it all. It would take time to readjust to normal food again.

Later that evening Jim went up to the deck and stood by the rail looking out toward the island in the distance that had claimed the lives of so many of his men. He remained on deck for several minutes, leaning against the rail in quiet retrospection. It had been a tough battle, but they had accomplished their mission. For that, he felt a measure of pride; he had done his duty. That pride, however, was tempered by the thought of the high number of casualties that had cost to achieve their mission. But had it been worth it? Had it been so necessary in the greater scheme of the war that some of the finest men he had ever known must die? He wrestled with these questions, but the answers eluded him. He took one last look at the silhouette of Iwo Jima, a place that had forever changed him, before slowly walking down to his cabin. For the first time in four weeks, he climbed into a bunk and lay on a soft mattress. As he drifted off to sleep, he thought to himself, "It's great to be alive."

That first night aboard ship he slept fitfully and dreamed about the battle. The next night the battle demons left him, and he slept undisturbed the rest of the way back to Hawaii.

7

Return to Camp Maui

Some people spend an entire lifetime wondering
if they made a difference in the world. But the
Marines don't have that problem.
—President Ronald Reagan, 1985

The return trip to Hawaii did not take as long as the trip to Iwo Jima. Although the threat was greatly reduced, there still was a Japanese submarine menace. Jim had very little in the way of responsibilities on the return trip, so he was able to relax. The best part of the entire trip back to Hawaii was "sack time." Because of Japanese harassing mortar fire, except during the last week on Iwo Jima, he rarely got to sleep through the night. Aboard ship he got as much sleep as he could. Eventually his stomach tolerated normal food, and he began to eat properly and to gain back some of the weight he had lost. When he came off Iwo Jima, his weight was down to 115 pounds.

Jim did have one responsibility during the cruise back to Hawaii. As platoon leader he had to write a letter to the next of kin on record of every Marine under his command who had been killed. This was not something that Jim dreaded; he took the responsibility seriously and spent a lot of time composing each letter. There was certain information about the dead Marine that he had to include, such as when and where he was killed and what kind of wound it was, but Jim did not stop with the required information. At the end of each letter he added a paragraph in which he described some unique characteristic about each man that would let the family know that he had indeed known their son or husband personally. Because he wrote each letter by hand, the time passed quickly. It also allowed Jim one last opportunity to recall each of the men in his platoon who had died. When he was finished, he had 20 letters.

They stopped for a day or two in the Marianas to take on supplies, then continued to Pearl Harbor where they dropped anchor off Ford Island. He took a launch to the dock and then enjoyed the freedom of a leisurely stroll along the streets and beaches of Waikiki. It was so nice to walk in the open without somebody shooting at him. Memories of Iwo Jima, however, were never very far from his consciousness, and the sting of death still haunted him.

One of the first places he went was the Moana Hotel dining room because he knew he could get milk there, something he had not tasted in weeks. He had a quiet dinner and savored the milk. It tasted heavenly. As he finished his dinner, a man walked up and asked if he might share his table. Jim motioned him to a chair, and he began talking about the war.

"Sounds like we got the Japs on the run. We'll be in Tokyo 'fore long, I expect. They can't last much longer."

"No, I don't suppose they can." Jim was curious to hear what the man had to say.

"Hey, did you read about this battle on Iwo Jima? I read in the papers that it was one hell of a fight."

Jim said nothing.

"I guess we really whipped them. But we paid a big price for it. I heard that we had over 25,000 casualties."

Jim was shocked. He had not heard this. He knew they had a lot of casualties, but he didn't know it had been that high.

"They say it was the bloodiest battle in the war. Hey, I also read where the Ruskies are closing in on Berlin."

The man continued talking, but Jim was no longer listening. He knew it had been bad, but he had no idea they had lost so many men. This was a stunning revelation. He paid for his dinner, excused himself, and left. He walked out into the warm sunshine and headed back to the ship. The next day the ship weighed anchor and sailed for Maui.

———•———

Over the course of the next several weeks, replacements arrived to fill in the depleted ranks. Jim was still a platoon leader, and the war was not yet over. He began training with them for the next operation, the invasion of Japan. The scuttlebutt circulating in camp was that the Marines and some of MacArthur's troops had invaded Okinawa and were involved in another bloody battle. When he found Okinawa on the map it did not take much to realize that the next step was Japan itself.

One day the entire division was called out to the parade ground for an official ceremony. Jim stood at rigid attention in front of 1st Platoon. The regimental commander, Col. Walter Jordan, presented medals to those of the 4th Division who had distinguished themselves on Iwo Jima. When it came time to present the Purple Heart medals, Jim was taken completely by surprise when his name was also called. The Purple Heart is awarded to members of the armed forces who are wounded by an instrument of war in the hands of the enemy and posthumously to the next of kin in the name of those who are killed in action or die of wounds received in action. Even though Jim had not reported his shrapnel wound, his men had. He, rightfully, was awarded this prestigious decoration. He stepped forward with the other Purple Heart recipients and stood ramrod straight as Jordan pinned it to his uniform.

After a few weeks of training, he received the only leave he was to get in the Marine Corps, a five-day pass in Waikiki. It took one day of his five days off to get from Camp Maui to Waikiki and one day to get back. While in Waikiki he and three others shared a room in a house near the beach. The day after they arrived, Jim ran into one of his men, Corporal Kistler. They caught up on events since they had last seen each other on Iwo Jima. Kistler knew Dick Crockett's aunt and uncle who lived in Honolulu, and said they might like to meet him. It was arranged, and they met the family at their home for dinner that evening. They were greeted warmly and asked about Dick's experiences in battle.

Jim was not used to this, but he gave an honest account. "Well, ma'am, sir, Dick was under my command. I was his platoon leader. He was well liked by everybody in the platoon, and I personally liked him. He was always willing to carry his share of the load. He wasn't scared any more than anybody else—we all were—but he was a brave man and a fine Marine. You have every reason to be very proud of your nephew. He was a credit to the Corps, and he died fighting for his country. I can't think of a better epitaph or a better cause."

"Can you tell us how Dick died?"

Jim described how Dick Crockett had run out of time trying to throw a Japanese grenade out of his foxhole. Dick's aunt and uncle had not heard this. Afterwards, they expressed their thanks to Jim for taking the time to come talk with them. After a few awkward moments, Jim and Kistler said good-bye and left.

The next day Jim visited the military hospital in Honolulu where, to his surprise, he ran into Lieutenants Walker and Ware. They were in the hospital recovering from wounds they had received on Iwo Jima.

With a big grin on his face, Walker said, "Hey, Jim, what are you doing here? We thought you were dead."

"Y'know, I've heard that before," he quipped. "Well, as you can see, I'm not. Not a scratch."

During the rest of the spring and summer Jim trained with his men, but the platoon was now composed of more new men than veterans. Some of the men who had been wounded had recovered and rejoined his platoon. They spent part of each day in "book learning" classes held outside sitting on the ground. Jim quizzed the new men about tactics, and if he was not satisfied with their answers, he would tell them to go look it up in the book.

He took the men out on long hikes through the hills and valleys of Camp Maui. The verdant vegetation and beautiful landscape were welcome sights after the ugly, featureless terrain of Iwo Jima. To Jim, these hikes were enjoyable, and he looked forward to them.

Occasionally Jim was given a couple of days off. He and seven buddies decided to go up to the crater of Haleakala, which, at 10,033 feet, was the highest point on the island. After requisitioning a couple of jeeps, they drove through the clouds along a winding road to the top of the crater rim. The easiest way to get to the bottom of the crater was to slide down the steep slope on their butts. Jim had a map that indicated some interesting features of the crater that he wanted to see. One was a mini-crater in a cone that went down into the belly of the volcano. He was curious about what was inside the cone. When he had found one he spent the next hour climbing to the top. When he reached the top he peered inside. What he saw was a big disappointment. There was nothing to see but a deep, dark hole.

By the time they finished exploring, it was dark. Because they were so high and the skies were so clear, they could see millions of stars. The Milky Way cut a swath across the sky, and a bright moon cast eerie shadows on the crater wall. They spent the night in one of two cabins inside the crater, and the next morning they watched the sun rise above the crater rim.

They wandered around on the crater floor for a few hours and came out along a worn path. Apparently a herd of goats used to come in and out of the crater the same way, eventually cutting a little path into the wall. The goat path followed a switchback course up the inside of the crater until it reached the rim, a vertical distance of about 3,000 feet. This path was quite narrow and dropped off steeply. In mountain climbing parlance, this path would be said to have high exposure. One of the tough men with Jim, though he may have been able to attack a heavily defended Japanese machine gun position, was deathly afraid of heights. He turned his back to the drop-off and inched his way to the top, never once looking down.

Located on the east side of the island, Hana was another favorite place to visit on days off. Jim and a few of his buddies drove there one day along the north shore, winding their way in and out of canyons, past lush fields, dense forests, and swaying palm trees. It was an idyllic setting. Jim and his buddies spent the afternoon swimming and relaxing in the sun. In this peaceful setting they could take their minds off the war and enjoy themselves.

———·—

There was no doubt that Japan was the next target, so Jim and his men continued to train. They spent most of their training on bivouacs rather than in the camp proper. Every evening a Marine with a field kitchen brought them their meals. On 7 August 1945, he brought some interesting news.

"Hey, Lieutenant, have you heard the scuttlebutt?"

"No, I haven't heard anything. In fact, I've not heard anything for several days. What's going on?"

"Well, the scuttlebutt is that we've dropped some kind of super bomb on Japan."

"Well, I haven't heard anything about a super bomb. It's probably just another rumor. Don't believe everything you hear." Jim did not think any more about it. In fact, he did not even mention it to his men. No use in getting their hopes up, he thought. It might be too distracting, and they still had to keep focused on their training.

The next day the same guy came back with their meals and said, "Y'know, Lieutenant, there may be something to this super bomb rumor. Now the scuttlebutt is that this may mean the end of the war." Still Jim was skeptical, but he passed the news along to his men.

On 10 August, they returned to camp. Every radio in the camp was on, and the news was that a second super bomb, now called an atomic bomb, had been dropped on Nagasaki. Rumors ran wild through the camp that this did indeed mean that the end of the war was imminent. Despite the rumors, Jim knew that he had to maintain unit discipline. He continued to take his men out on long hikes and to train them in battlefield tactics.

During the night of 15 August, Jim was lying on his cot. He thought he heard somebody shouting, and he strained to hear. A few seconds later he distinctly heard someone shouting, "The war's over." He got up and walked over to the officers' mess tent. Everybody was crowded around a radio. The news was not that the war was over but that Radio Tokyo had gone off the air and was just playing martial music. An official announcement was expected at any time. It was not until a couple of days later that the Marines got the official word that the war was indeed over. Following this announcement, there was a noticeable spike in morale. The men were more relaxed, but they were still Marines and they had to continue training.

On 2 September 1945, the Japanese signed the surrender document on board the USS *Missouri* in Tokyo Bay. (A peace treaty was not signed until 1951, officially ending the war between Japan and the United States.) There would be no invasion of Japan, but neither would there be a mass demobilization with everybody going home at once. The Marines had a point system whereby those with enough points were the first ones sent home to be discharged. Points were accumulated based on the length of service and the number of campaigns one had fought in. Marines in the 4th Division who had fought on Roi-Namur, Saipan, and Tinian in addition to Iwo Jima had the most points and were the first to be sent home. Since Iwo Jima had been Jim's only campaign, he was obligated to remain in the Marines until those who had served longer were discharged.

The 3rd Battalion had suffered so many casualties on Iwo Jima that for all practical purposes it had ceased to exist as an effective fighting unit. What was left of the battalion was formed into the 9th Military Police Battalion. Jim became an official military policeman. After a few weeks someone discovered that he did not have a military driver's license. He could not be an MP without a license. He and several others in the same predicament were sent to the camp mess hall to take a written test. They were not given any time to prepare for the test nor were they told what was going to be on it. They were just told to show up. Everyone flunked the test. A few days later, they were issued military driver's licenses anyway. Apparently the Marines had ways to get around bothersome rules.

Those who were not sent home and who were not assigned to the Military Police Battalion were assigned to help tear down Camp Maui. Jim regretted not getting this duty. If he had, he would have sent for Pat. It could have been the honeymoon they had missed. But the Marines did not ask him what assignment he wanted. They just gave him an order, and he saluted and gave them the only response: "Aye, aye, sir."

One day Jim received orders that he was to ship out the next day for duty as an MP. He was on his way to Okinawa—practically Japan itself.

8

Occupation Duty

The best duty I ever had.
—2nd Lt. James Craig

Before he left for Okinawa in November 1945, Jim and some of his officer buddies went down to a dump where some old furniture from the now dismantled Camp Maui lay discarded. He found some cross-legged folding chairs and helped himself to one. He took his chair with him on board the transport and lounged in it on deck every day that the weather permitted.

With the war over, there was no longer a need for the precautionary zigzag pattern. This time the trip across the Pacific was shorter. In contrast to the trip to Iwo Jima, this voyage was leisurely; Jim had time to rest and read.

The building of the atomic bomb and the consideration for its use against Japan was such a closely held secret that only a select few in the higher echelons of the military knew of its existence. Planning for the eventual invasion of Japan, code-named Operation Downfall, continued even after the bombs were dropped, right up until Japan accepted the terms of surrender on 15 August 1945. Had it been necessary to invade Japan, Okinawa was to have served as the jumping-off point for American forces. Lying 400 miles south of Kyushu, Okinawa was essential to the American plans. The invasion of Okinawa began on 1 April 1945, and the island was declared secure on 22 June. Once Okinawa was secured, tons of supplies and munitions began arriving in preparation for the planned invasion. Thousands of civilians were rounded up and placed in a rehabilitation center until their homes could be rebuilt. The 9th Military Police (MP)

Battalion was sent to Okinawa to provide security for the American base and the rehabilitation center.

The U.S. occupation forces divided Okinawa into three districts. The 9th Military Police Battalion was assigned to one of these districts. Jim and his platoon were given responsibility for a rehabilitation center in one of three subdistricts within his battalion's district. As a second lieutenant, he was the highest-ranking MP in this subdistrict. His primary responsibility was to maintain the peace and security at the rehabilitation center where the displaced citizens lived. The poor Okinawans, as so often happens in war, were nonbelligerent civilians caught in the middle. They suffered thousands of casualties, and nearly all of them lost their homes.

Looking north from Ishikawa, Jim could see the little island of Ie Shima, where the Hoosier war correspondent Ernie Pyle was killed by a Japanese sniper on 18 April 1945.

Initially, the U.S. Army provided security for the area, and it continued in this capacity for two weeks after the Marines arrived. During this overlap period, Jim had a chance to observe the Army checkpoint at the entrance to the rehab center. One of the first things he noticed was the work detail that drove trucks into the village to pick up Okinawan laborers. Jim had been instructed that nobody was allowed into the village without proper *written* authorization, yet the trucks seemed to come and go without anybody stopping them to check for this authorization.

The compound, especially the village where the civilians lived, was off-limits to all military personnel without proper authorization. At night Jim heard screams from inside the village and saw soldiers from the work battalion, located just down the road, sneaking in and out of the compound. He suspected they were harassing and raping the women.

Jim was issued a broken-down jeep to patrol the roads. Unfortunately, it would only go the prescribed 35-mph speed limit. One day his men stopped a speeding truck. When they asked the driver for his authorization papers, three men in the back jumped out with machine guns and demanded to be allowed to pass. As MPs they were only issued .45-caliber pistols. A pistol is no match for a machine gun, and he had learned on Iwo Jima not to argue with anyone holding a machine gun. They let the truck pass.

Jim soon discovered that most of the military vehicles on the island were not properly registered. He and his men set up checkpoints and started checking for proper registration and comparing the vehicle registration number against a list of stolen vehicles. He was surprised how many had been stolen. When he came across a stolen vehicle, he confiscated it. Some of the men in his battalion were good mechanics, and they fixed up the confiscated jeeps and painted them to look like Marine jeeps. Before long, the Marine MP Battalion had a nice fleet of jeeps that would go over 35 mph.

On the morning his platoon of MPs was to take over security, he saw a long line of military trucks backed up in front of the gate to the village waiting to get in. His men were not allowing any vehicle to enter that did not have proper authorization, and he intended to make sure that rules were obeyed. Discipline would be maintained, even if it had not been before.

He had no doubt about what to expect when he got to his office. An Army officer came by and demanded to see who was in charge. It was obvious that he was not there for a friendly chat. He outranked Jim by several grades. This would be the first test of his authority.

An army major (three ranks above him) stomped up to him, looked him squarely in the eye, and said in a gruff voice, "Who's in charge here?"

Jim came to attention, saluted, and said, "I am, sir."

"And just who the hell are you?"

"Second Lieutenant James Craig, United States Marine Corps, sir."

"Why aren't you letting my men in to collect their work details from this village?"

"Sir, they do not have proper authorization, and unless they can show proper authorization, I cannot let them in."

"They're working for me, and I told them to go in and collect the work detail. That ought to be all the authorization you need."

"Sir, unless they have *written* authorization, I will not let them pass."

"Do you realize that I am a major in the United States Army?"

"Yes, sir. But I have my orders, and those orders state that no one without proper written authorization is to be allowed into the village, sir."

"You mean to tell me that you are not going to allow my men to go in and collect their work detail?"

The major was becoming irate. Jim knew he was in the right, and this stiffened his resolve not to cave in to the major's intimidating posture and implied threat. "Yes, sir. That is correct. When they show me the proper written authorization, I will be more than happy to allow them in, but until then, no . . . sir." Jim stood as erect as he could and kept his eyes fixed straight ahead. He was rather enjoying this, but kept a smile to himself.

The major towered over Jim. He got as close as he could, practically nose-to-nose with him, and said, "You listen to me, *lieutenant*. I want your name, rank, and serial number. We'll see who's in charge here."

Jim did not flinch. In a loud clear voice he intoned, "Sir, Craig, James, second lieutenant, 041794, sir." He shouted the last *sir*.

The major did not even bother writing it down. It was obvious that his bluff was not going to work. As his parting shot he growled, "You'll be hearing from me," and stormed off, leaving Jim standing there with a smile on his face.

The next day the same trucks started showing up with the proper written authorization for entry into the village to collect their work details, and they were allowed in without argument. Those without authorization were turned back. Discipline had been reestablished.

Periodically the MPs would perform "shakedowns," unannounced searches of the men's barracks designed to find and collect unauthorized weapons. Apparently the army did these shakedowns but collected few contraband weapons. This changed when the Marines took over as MPs. Jim's men performed several "shakedowns" and confiscated a substantial collection of rifles and pistols that were not registered.

Within a few weeks things simmered down and there was less trouble. Jim no longer heard screaming at night, and nobody entered the village without authorization.

———·———

Not all women were afraid of sexual advances by American soldiers, as long as conditions were right. One day three young Okinawan women came to Jim with a request. With the aid of an interpreter, they asked for permission to open a brothel in the village. They were not sluts. Their appearance and demeanor were no different than all the other Okinawan women Jim had seen. Sex for hire was apparently much more accepted in Japanese culture than in Western culture, but Jim denied their request anyway. There would be no open prostitution for Marines in his subdistrict as long as he was in charge.

———·———

One evening Jim and his sergeant, David Cohen, were walking along the road between his barracks and the village. They came upon an overturned jeep on the side of the road. Two soldiers from the Army work battalion stood nearby, but when he questioned them about the accident, they denied that they were involved. Since nobody else was around, Jim suspected they were lying. As an MP Jim had the authority to arrest the two men on suspicion of theft, and he did so. He and Cohen took the two men back to their camp to turn them over to their battalion commander.

Word spread throughout the camp. When Jim and Cohen emerged from the commander's quarters, several members of the work battalion gathered around the barracks and looked menacing. They barred the way out of camp and then surrounded Jim and Cohen. To get out they would have to pass through the mob. Jim recognized the threat and decided to go on the offensive. Without hesitation he pulled out his .45-caliber pistol and, pointing it at no one in particular, said in a loud voice, "You sons of bitches get back in your tents right now. This is none of your damn business. Now move, or I'm going to start shooting." When confronted by this authoritarian posture, the men backed down and retreated to their tents. Jim and Cohen left without any trouble, and Jim never heard any more about it. He had established his authority, and from that point on it was respected.

———•——

Although it was not an official part of his responsibilities, as the highest-ranking MP he was expected to make an appearance in the village periodically. Once a day he walked down the streets simply to be seen. By now Jim had become accepted in the village. The Okinawans bowed respectfully as he walked by. They knew that after the Marines arrived, the soldiers stopped sneaking into their village and that he was responsible for the improved conditions.

Every Sunday the Okinawans performed local folk music on an open air stage. The show usually lasted all day. Out of respect Jim attended these performances and stayed for an hour or two, always arriving during the middle of the show. When he walked into the audience, the music came to an abrupt halt and all the Okinawans stood in deferential respect. Once he was seated, the Okinawans sat down and the show continued.

———•——

Many of the Okinawan women went bare-breasted, and those who wore a shirt usually wore it open with little regard for western modesty. Perhaps this cultural difference excited some of the men in the work battalion, who chased the women until the Marines took over security. Another manifestation of this cultural difference was the way in which the Okinawans behaved around the latrine. In the latrine there was a pipe with a funnel attached to the top for a urinal. There was also a wooden seat to sit on over a hole in the ground. When Marines used the latrine, some of the Okinawan women might be inside cleaning, but nobody thought anything of it. It was a little hard to get used to at first, but it was not long before the Marines, including Jim, accepted it as just the way things were. It was the same way at the latrine in the village. Women sat on a wooden seat next to the men as people walked by, and nobody took any notice of it.

When the latrines filled to capacity, an Okinawan work detail would "dip the honey" out and dump it into a two-wheeled cart affectionately called the "honey wagon." Jim never knew where they took the waste, and he really did not care to know. It only mattered that somebody took it away. One day a wagon wheel broke off. The wagon tilted so that its contents spilled out right next to the sentry post outside the gate to the village. The stench was so overwhelming that Jim had to relieve the men standing guard frequently until the mess was cleaned up.

———·——

Every day a woman and her two young nieces came to clean up around Jim's tent. They each had only two sets of clothes: a dress that they had before their home was destroyed and a set of dungarees given to them by the Marines. One day they wore their dresses, and the next day they wore the Marine dungarees. Every day when they came to work, Jim noticed how neat their clothes were. They obviously laundered and ironed them daily. He was impressed. Although they were living in a makeshift refugee camp, after losing their homes and nearly all of their worldly possessions, they still retained a quiet dignity.

Toward the end of his stay on Okinawa, Jim and his interpreter requisitioned a jeep and drove the three women back to their home south of Naha, the capital of Okinawa. Once a modern city, Naha had been reduced to rubble during the invasion. When Jim arrived in their village, he was stunned by the devastation. The women's home was in the early stages of reconstruction when they arrived. As Jim and his interpreter were saying good-bye and preparing to leave, the women presented Jim with a gift. They had obtained a Marine blanket and, with the aid of a photograph, had tailored him an Eisenhower jacket, the shortened version of the standard Army jacket that the general had made so popular. It could not have been more professional looking had it been issued by the U.S. Army. Jim was moved by their generosity and immediately put it on. He wore his Eisenhower jacket with pride. It represented a peace offering of sorts. It was their way of thanking Jim for the kindness he had shown them. The healing process had begun with that simple gesture.

———·——

Ed Cavalini, Jim's friend from Camp Pendleton, was an MP on a different part of Okinawa. They both received orders in early February that they were to be relieved. A few days later, they boarded the transport ship that took them home.

9

Going Home

And when he gets to Heaven
To St. Peter he will tell:
"One more Marine reporting, Sir—
I've served my time in Hell."
—Sgt. James A. Donahue, USMC

The return trip to the States in February 1946 was a direct one with no stop in Hawaii. En route the Marines were informed that they would be quarantined for three days upon arrival in San Francisco, where they would be searched and subject to an inspection overseen by the Army. Jim had picked up an M1 rifle on Iwo Jima that he wanted to take home with him as a souvenir. After all, he figured he had earned it. But the Army could not let all the men who were being discharged take their weapons home with them. They were, after all, the property of Uncle Sam. The promised inspection in San Francisco would find him out, and he would have to relinquish his prize. Still, there was a chance he might somehow smuggle it in, since it might be overlooked during the inspection. Unfortunately, he lost his nerve and tossed the rifle overboard.

Early on the day they were to pull into San Francisco Bay, Ed Cavalini, a native of San Francisco, roused Jim. "We're almost there. You gotta come up on deck and see the bridge. If there isn't any fog, it's one hell of a sight."

They quickly dressed and went up on deck. It was still dark and also, to their disappointment, very foggy. Ed said, "We've just passed the Farallon Islands, so we're getting close to the bay." They went to the front of the ship but could see nothing. Suddenly the fog parted and the Golden Gate Bridge loomed directly above them. All Jim could say was "Wow!"

Shortly after they arrived, he left his prized cross-legged chair and went to check in. When he returned a few minutes later, his chair was gone. He really liked that chair and wanted to take it back to Pendleton, but, he mused to himself, if that was all he lost in this war, then that was all right.

The Army was in charge of the quarantine, but an hour after they had docked, a contingent of Marines came aboard and escorted the passengers off the ship. There was no quarantine and no inspection. How Jim wished he had kept that M1. They were put up in a hotel for four days until transportation home could be arranged.

As the train traveled over the snow-covered Rockies and across the wide, monotonous expanse of the Great Plains, Jim could think of nothing but seeing Pat again. He had not seen her for 15 months, and they were still newlyweds as far as he was concerned. The train from San Francisco took him to Chicago, where he had to dash from Union Station to another station several blocks away to catch the train to Indianapolis. He didn't have time to call Pat.

Jim knew the route the train was supposed to take, but it took an unexpected detour, which delayed his scheduled arrival time by several hours. As he got off the train, his first inclination was to find a phone and call Pat. He walked into the lobby and found her waiting there. She had been at the station to meet every train coming in from Chicago that day. She ran to him. He dropped his bag and enfolded her into his arms. Their first kiss made up for all the others they had missed.

After spending one night in an Indianapolis hotel, they drove to Pendleton. Jim was still in the Marines, so he wore the Eisenhower jacket the Okinawan women had made for him. One of the first things his dad asked was, "Well, how are the Japs?" Jim danced around the question without really answering him. Much later he realized that his dad probably wanted to talk about Iwo Jima. He regrets not talking to his dad about his experience.

He changed into his dungarees and went down to his dad's lumberyard. There were no "Welcome home, hero" signs, slaps on the back, or any other indications that people knew he was home. He quietly melted back into small-town society. He had been away for a number of years to Westtown, Purdue, various training camps, and then the war, and many people had forgotten him.

In March 1946 he got a notice from the Marines that he was eligible for separation if he so chose. The separation process in Chicago took a few days, and during this time the Marines tried to talk Jim into staying in the Marine Reserves. As much as Jim liked the Marines, he had other plans. If a war broke out in the next few years, there was no question in his mind that he would get his commission and become a rifle platoon leader again.

Of the 30 or so other Marines who were eligible for separation in his group, only Jim and another man opted out. The rest joined the Reserves. In 1950 the North Korean army invaded South Korea and dragged the United States into war again. Marine reservists were among the first to go into battle. Some were bitter, but as Jim pointed out, they had had their chance to get out, just as he had.

As a little slap on the wrist for not staying in the Reserves, Jim was demoted from lieutenant to sergeant, but it was not just from a second lieutenant that he was demoted. While he was on terminal leave waiting for the option to separate from the Marines, they had promoted him to first lieutenant.

10

War and Valor

In war: resolution.
In defeat: defiance.
In victory: magnanimity.
In peace: good will.
—Winston Churchill

An account of the battle of Iwo Jima would be incomplete without a summary of casualty figures. Of the more than 70,000 Marines of the three divisions of the 5th Amphibious Corps who fought on Iwo Jima, over one-third of them, 25,851, were casualties. To put this in perspective, this number represents roughly the equivalent of over an entire Marine division. This number includes 5,931 killed and missing in action, 17,272 wounded, and 2,648 battle fatigue cases. (Total U.S. casualties during the battle, including those of the Navy and Army, was 28,686. This total includes the often quoted figure of 6,821 killed and 19,217 wounded.) Of the 4th Marine Division's 9,098 casualties, 1,806 were killed or listed as missing in action, including 92 officers, and 7,292 were wounded. There is one other sobering casualty statistic that is worth noting. Of all the Marines killed during World War II, including all the island campaigns in the Pacific, one-third were killed on Iwo Jima.

Of the estimated 21,000 Japanese defenders on Iwo Jima, only 216 survived and were taken prisoner. Many of these survivors were Korean laborers.

Jim landed on Iwo Jima on 19 February 1945 with 41 men of the 1st Platoon. During the course of the battle 19 Marines were added to his platoon as replacements. Of the 60 Marines under his command during the 28 days he was on Iwo Jima, 20 were killed and 30 suffered wounds that required evacuation. After four weeks of brutal combat, Jim walked off the island with only 10 of his men. This represents an 83 percent casualty rate. As a functioning combat unit, 1st Platoon had virtually ceased to exist.

This account would be incomplete without some mention of the use of the atomic bombs. The Japanese fought with increasing ferocity as the Marines got closer to the Home Islands, and with their Bushido philosophical approach to war, there was little doubt that the Japanese would continue to fight. Their stubbornness and belligerence would necessitate invading Japan to end the war. Had there been an invasion of Japan, which Jim was training for at the time the two atomic bombs were dropped, there was a high probability that he would not have survived it. Following the surrender of Germany in May 1945, U.S. Army units were en route to the Pacific to take part in the invasion. Some estimates of the number of American casualties during an invasion of Japan ran as high as 1 million with an equal number of Japanese casualties. This staggering figure would exceed the battle casualties suffered by all U.S. armed forces in World War II. Comparing these casualty estimates with the death toll from the atomic bombings of Hiroshima and Nagasaki makes the case for the use of the bombs. The atomic bombs shortened the war and saved thousands of lives, both Japanese and American. Every Marine veteran with whom I've spoken was in favor of using the atomic bombs on Japan.

I must comment on the dilemma that Jim faced when he chose to ignore Lieutenant Makowski's initial order to advance on D+19. In my opinion it was the most courageous act of the many that Jim performed on Iwo Jima. If Makowski had continued to insist that Jim advance and if Jim had just as stubbornly refused, he would have committed a court-martial offense. I can only speculate about what was going through Makowski's mind at the time. Fortunately for Jim and his men, Makowski must have concluded that Jim did indeed have a better understanding of the tactical situation and was right in halting the advance. I must hasten to add that Makowski demonstrated equal strength of character when he acquiesced and tacitly rescinded his order by not further insisting that Jim advance, thereby diffusing a potentially indefensible situation for Jim. He was spared the anguish of making an impossible decision, that of disobeying a direct lawful order of a superior officer or violating his conscience.

The Uniform Code of Military Justice is clear regarding the failure to obey a lawful order. Under Article 90, paragraph 4.14.1 a, "Any person . . . who . . . willfully disobeys a lawful command of his superior commissioned officer shall be punished, if the offense is committed in time of war, by death or such other punishment as a court-martial may direct." Paragraph

4.14.3 c. (2) (iii) puts to rest any confusion surrounding the lawfulness of the order and the influence of a man's conscience or personal beliefs as a justification for his disobedience. Under section (iii) it states: "The order must relate to military duty, which includes all activities reasonably necessary to accomplish a military mission. . . . The order may not, without such a valid military purpose, interfere with private rights or personal affairs. However, the dictates of a person's conscience, religion, or personal philosophy cannot justify or excuse the disobedience of an otherwise lawful order."

What was at stake for Jim if Makowski had insisted that his order be carried out? Whether or not it was a bad order is irrelevant. Makowski's order was indeed a lawful order. Therefore, Jim was duty bound to obey it, even if it violated his conscience. If Makowski persisted and ordered Jim to continue the advance and Jim chose to willfully disobey the order because he thought it would mean certain death for his men, he would have been doing so with the full knowledge of his actions and the consequences.

When confronted with a decision with equally distasteful outcomes, a man must act according to his conscience even if it means he must suffer the consequences, in this case the real possibility of a general court-martial. This was exactly the position adopted by the Allies during the Nuremberg War Crimes Tribunal—a man is morally responsible for his actions. It took great courage for Jim to stand his ground and do what he thought was right for his men. A lesser man might have taken the easy route, acquiesced, and done what he had been told to do, to the peril of his men. In my opinion, this was an example of heroic conviction. But nobody gets a medal for this kind of heroism.

———·—·———

Jim suggested that I set this story apart from the rest of the narrative to honor a particular member of 1st Platoon. Jim deeply regretted the loss of any of his men, but this Marine's death was somehow more poignant. The circumstances surrounding his death are forever burned into Jim's memory. Each time he recounted this story he would choke up, so moved was he by the life and death of Cpl. Jewel "Red" Bennett, who died on Sunday, 25 February 1945, on the ugliest place on the face of the earth.

The skies were leaden and the air was cool on Sunday morning, D+6. The men of 1st Platoon sat crouched in their foxholes waiting for the preparatory artillery and mortar barrage to be lifted before they stepped out and began the advance. They had already suffered several casualties since landing on the beach a few days earlier. Some of their buddies had been killed and others had been severely wounded. Once the barrage was lifted, they were all to get up and begin moving forward into enemy territory, not knowing which one of them would be the next to fall to a Japanese sniper's bullet or mortar shell.

Off to the right Jim noticed that Red was approaching his foxhole, and it was obvious he wanted to talk about something. Jim motioned for Red to come over and join him.

This was Red's fourth combat operation. He had fought on Roi-Namur, Saipan, and Tinian. During these campaigns he had managed to survive while many of his buddies had not. He explained to Jim that he thought his luck had run out and that he was not going to make it this time. He said that he had already apologized to the rest of the platoon for holding back and for not being the Marine that he was expected to be. He also wanted to apologize to his platoon leader.

Red was no coward. He never turned tail and ran in the face of enemy fire. But each morning when the platoon stepped out of their foxholes and began to advance, he was never the first one, where he would be more exposed; he remained back a little. He told Jim that this really bothered him. During the night, while sitting alone in his foxhole, he had prayed to God for courage to do his duty, and God had answered his prayer. Afterward Red said he no longer had any fear about what lay ahead for him. Whatever happened was God's will, and that was okay with him.

Jim was touched by this testimony. Before Red left to return to his foxhole, Jim saw that his bearing was one of peaceful resignation. Live or die, he was at peace because he knew that God alone controlled his fate.

Red had gone no more than 20 yards when a Japanese mortar shell landed at his feet and detonated. At that same instant a ray of sunlight broke through the early morning mist and penetrated the green smoke from the exploded mortar shell and illuminated his crumpled body. Stunned, Jim looked over at Red's body in anguish and had an epiphany. It was as if the ray of light was providing the way to heaven for the soul of Red Bennett.

Jim reflected on what Red had told him not two minutes earlier: "Whatever happens to me is God's will, and that's okay with me." Red died at peace with himself that morning because he knew that God had taken away his fear.

In telling this story Jim goes on to recite from John 15:13: "Greater love hath no man than this, that a man lay down his life for his friends." Sadly, thousands of men did just that in World War II. Red willingly went off to war when his country called, and he paid the ultimate price. For Jim it was paradoxical, for he had seen the glory of God that morning in a place that was very nearly hell itself.

Epilogue: Iwo Jima, 14 March 2002

Our chartered plane lifted off the runway on Guam and climbed into the predawn sky. Looking into the inky blackness I imagined that we would be flying the same course the B-29s had flown on their way to bomb Japan in 1945. Along their way they would have flown over Iwo Jima. Today several Marines who had survived the battle on Iwo Jima in 1945 were returning for one last look. There were also many family members of those who had fought on Iwo Jima. One man was only five years old when his father was killed in the battle, and he had come to find the spot where his father had died. A woman wanted to see where her father, a member of the Navy Construction Battalion, had helped build the airfields on Iwo Jima after the Marines had secured it. There was a Navy corpsman who wanted to see where he had treated the wounded and the dying. The oldest veteran in our group was 89, and the highest-ranking veteran was a retired major general. They all had their own reasons for returning.

My reason for going was simple. I wanted to see where my uncle Jim Craig had fought. After all the work I had put into writing his story, all the reading and research and interviews, it was only fitting that I, too, should see Iwo Jima for myself. When I serendipitously stumbled onto the Military Historical Tours website advertising the 57th Anniversary Reunion of Honor tour, I was drawn to Iwo Jima like a magnet.

As I settled into my seat for the two-hour flight I considered my august traveling companions. They were the very men who had fought alongside Jim during those four fateful weeks in 1945. These were the Marines—many mere boys at the time—who had placed themselves in harm's way to defend freedom and American ideals.

The anxious anticipation in the cabin of the plane was almost palpable. I knew that it would be an emotional experience to stand on the beaches where so much blood had been shed, where so many Marines had died violently and where more than 20,000 Japanese soldiers had died. This was not only a reunion of American Marine veterans. This was also a reunion of Japanese veterans. Marine veterans would be meeting what few Japanese veterans were still alive. Fifty-seven years ago they met on Iwo Jima as mortal enemies. Today they were coming to meet in peace and to reconcile old animosities.

A stewardess collected our passports, which would be returned when we boarded the plane for the return to Guam later tonight with an Iwo Jima/Japan visa stamp—a highly coveted souvenir.

Before 1945 Iwo Jima was part of Japan, specifically the Tokyo Prefecture. After the war the United States occupied the island until 1968, when it was ceded back to Japan as part of a treaty. That treaty stipulates that U.S. Marines can use the island for training purposes. It also states that World War II Marine veterans can return to the island once a year. There are no hotels and no tourist amenities on the island; it is a Japanese military base.

The sun slowly rose on the eastern horizon to illuminate the endless expanse of the Pacific Ocean. I looked down on the placid surface of the blue water and wondered what it must have been like for the Marines 57 years ago, crammed on troop transports heading for their date with destiny. It seemed incongruous that the Pacific should look so peaceful as we neared the island where the Marine Corps fought the bloodiest battle in its history. The dawn of D-Day had also been clear, very much like it was today.

The pilot informed us of the procedure we were to follow once we landed. A contingent of U.S. Marines would be lined up to formally greet us. Maj. Gen. Fred Haynes, a veteran of the 28th Marines, would have the honor of being the first person off the plane, followed by the rest of the Iwo Jima veterans, then other World War II veterans, and lastly the families of veterans.

As we rounded Mount Suribachi, white fumes coming from the crater reminded me that this volcano is still dormant. Iwo Jima was much smaller than I had envisioned. I was also surprised by how green it looked. Up until my first glimpse of the island, my impressions had been formed by World War II documentaries, which gave me a false sense of its size. They also depicted the island as barren and completely devoid of vegetation. During the flight from Guam we were told that planes flew over Iwo Jima after the war and bombed the entire island with seeds so that today, in sharp contrast to 1945, it is overgrown with bushes and trees.

The pilot flew out over the water again and turned parallel to the east coast so that we had a perfect view of the landing beaches. I easily picked out Blue 1 and 2, the section of the beach where Uncle Jim had landed. The pilot circled Mount Suribachi one more time to line us up for the easterly approach to the runway. As we touched down, the passengers cheered.

I found it hard to believe that I was on an island where 90,000 combatants had fired millions of rounds of mortar shells, artillery shells, and bullets. We taxied to the terminal past several jet fighters parked next to hangers. On the main terminal tower, the American and Japanese national flags fluttered in the breeze.

After the veterans deplaned, the family members followed. About 100 Marines stood at ease in two rows forming a passageway for us to walk along.

We lingered on the tarmac talking and taking photographs before we were ushered to waiting Humvees. Marines drove us to the 40th anniversary memorial overlooking the landing beaches. We passed what I imagined to be the amphitheater, Turkey Knob, and Charlie Dog Ridge. These features had long since been obliterated in the process of constructing the airfield. A golf course now lay on the spot where the amphitheater used to be.

As we drove along the dusty dirt road, I tried to imagine what it must have been like for the entrenched Japanese to look at the same scene. What must they have thought in the dawn of 19 February 1945 when they first saw the enormous military armada standing offshore and watched wave upon wave of landing craft churning toward them?

After a short ride we came to a halt by some tents on each side of the memorial. It appeared that well over 100 Marines were clustered around the memorial, some standing at rigid attention under one of the tents. They were all dressed in their camouflaged uniforms.

One tent had been erected for the many American and Japanese dignitaries and guests, many of whom were already greeting one another. In the middle of a clearing stood a cairn of stones with a plaque with the inscribed words "40th Anniversary Memorial and Reunion of Honor." A Marine band played martial music while Japanese men prepared for some kind of memorial rite.

I was introduced to an elderly Japanese whom I was informed was a survivor of the battle. He then greeted one of the survivors from our group, and they shook hands and, in a gesture of friendship, exchanged caps.

From pictures in some of the books I read about Iwo Jima I immediately recognized Taro Kuribayashi, son of Lt. Gen. Tadamichi Kuribayashi, the commander of the Japanese garrison during the battle.

Eventually the ceremony began with too many speeches, which had to be translated into Japanese and English. There was a long and, frankly, boring tea ceremony and a demonstration of Kendo, a Japanese sword fight. Afterwards, I laid a wreath on the 40th Reunion Memorial in memory of the men of Jim's platoon. I then ate a box lunch with two of the Marines from Okinawa. They looked so young, yet they were probably no different than the young Marines who stormed the beaches below us in 1945. I thought to myself, America's defense has been entrusted to the very best. In light of the ongoing war against terrorism, I felt confident that men such as these Marines would acquit themselves on the field of battle with distinction as their predecessors had done.

Time was passing quickly and there was much I wanted to see, not the least of which were the landing beaches and Mount Suribachi. Several of our group had already taken off for the summit of Suribachi as I started down to the landing beaches. The ceremony had taken place just above what I imagined to be the very center of the beaches, somewhere between where the 4th and 5th Divisions had landed.

I followed a path down through some scrub brush to a concrete bunker overlooking the beach and stopped to look inside. There was a back entrance away from the beach and a large aperture in front. Inside, a rusty Japanese Nambu light machine gun was fixed to the floor, directed toward the beach. I tried to imagine what it must have been like for the Japanese defenders inside this bunker enfilading the attacking Marines, knowing that eventually they must be overrun. They would have known of Kuribayashi's order to kill 10 Marines before they themselves were killed. I also tried to imagine what it was like for the advancing Marines when they came upon this well-defended bunker. This could very well have been the kind of position that Uncle Jim and his men encountered on numerous occasions as they advanced inland. They most likely would not have seen it until they were fired upon. Then they would have hit the deck and crawled for any kind of cover, most likely a shell hole. Jim would have made some assessment of the situation, then called back for "Smokey Bear" to bring up a machine gun squad. With the machine gun providing suppressing fire, Jim and his men would have worked around to the sides to outflank the Japanese position and attack it with grenades and rifle fire. As hard as I tried, I still could not fully appreciate the fear that both sides must surely have experienced.

The beach was wide and gently sloped to the water's edge. The terraces that the Marines crawled up were much further from the water than I imagined. I picked up a handful of sand and was surprised to find that it was not really sand at all but rather a loose, coarse gravel. And it was indeed black. It was easy to understand why it was so difficult to dig a foxhole in it. One of the things I wanted to bring back from Iwo Jima was a sample of the sand. We had been told that there was no limit to the amount we could collect. I filled two liter bottles full and stored them in my backpack.

As I surveyed the beaches, from the East Boat Basin in the north to the slopes of Mount Suribachi in the south, I again tried to imagine the battle.

On the morning of D-Day, thousands of Marines crawled and huddled on these very beaches. Bullets were flying, shells exploding, and men dying. Blood congealed with the sand, and body parts were plastered to the sides of shell holes. The cacophony of explosions, men's screams, and gunfire would have been heard up and down the beach. The smell would have been one of burnt cordite and burnt flesh—the smell of death. Beached landing craft, disabled tanks, and other accoutrements of amphibious warfare littered the beach. Dead Marines would be everywhere, some floating in the surf.

I pushed this scene from my mind and continued down toward the water's edge. I passed a young Japanese man coming up, and we stopped to talk. I know no Japanese, but his English was good enough that we could understand each other. I told him my uncle had fought here, and he told me that his grandfather had died here. We took each other's photograph, shook hands, and parted. There was much yet to see, so I quickly snapped photos of the beaches and the requisite photo of Mount Suribachi as I had seen it in books. I looked up to the looming volcano's silhouette and imagined the concentrated fire from well-concealed positions in its slopes raining down on the exposed Marines.

I walked back up to the road, climbed into a Humvee, and rode to the summit. During the short ride I had a pleasant conversation with the driver, a young woman from Hobart, Indiana. Before the war there was no road to the summit. Today a paved road snakes its way along the steep slopes to the top. During the short drive I imagined that we were passing caves and gun emplacements now hidden by the thick overgrowth of bushes. It was an eerie feeling. After we parked, I walked the last bit to the top.

From over 560 feet above the surf I looked down on the beaches just as the Japanese defenders would have seen them when the Marines landed in 1945. It must have been hard to wait, so tempting were the targets. They couldn't miss. When the beaches were crammed with Marines, they finally opened fire with their machine guns and preregistered mortars. The Marines had been sitting ducks.

There is a memorial marker near where the flag was raised in 1945. I found the spot and pondered the cost in blood to secure this part of the island. The flag that Joe Rosenthal photographed was raised on the northern rim of Suribachi. His photo gives the impression that the flag raisers are on the top of the mountain surrounded by a jumble of rocks and sticks. That part of the mountain is now flat, and grass grows around the paved road. The slope drops quickly toward the beaches on the north side, and the south side opens into a large crater. I walked around to the eastern rim of the crater and looked inside. Fumes rose from an unseen vent in the side of the crater, and the characteristic "rotten egg" smell of hydrogen sulfide was unmistakable.

I proceeded around the rim of the crater as far as I could go, then returned to the Humvee for the trip back down. While I waited, I took in the scene of the western beaches. These were the alternate landing beaches. Clearly visible in the distance was Kangoku Rock, the little island that Uncle Jim and his platoon were to take before H-Hour if the landings had taken place on the western side of the island. Kama Rock was also visible, but its appearance is distinctly different today than it was in 1945. Clearly an island in 1945, today it is the westernmost point of a peninsula jutting out from Iwo Jima. The entire island has been rising out of the sea.

I was again struck by how small the island is. It was difficult to imagine that over 90,000 combatants somehow fit on the island. Another feature was the narrow neck of the island just below Mount Suribachi. General Haynes told us that the men of the 28th Marines took only 90 minutes to reach the other side after they had landed. In only an hour and a half the Marines had cut the island in two, isolating Mount Suribachi.

As I waited for the next ride down, I stood on the top of Mount Suribachi and took in the scene below me. Birds chirped, the wind blew gently, and the sun warmed my face. The sky was blue with a few scattered clouds, and the waters of the calm Pacific washed up on the black beaches, breaking into white foam. It must have looked just like this the morning of D-Day before the Marines smashed ashore and the Japanese defenders opened fire, turning this peaceful scene into a living hell.

Notes

1. Prelude to War

1. Toland, *The Rising Sun*, 212.

2. Young, *First Twenty-four Hours of War in the Pacific*, ix.

3. This landing took place 80 minutes before the bombs began falling on Pearl Harbor, and so, strictly speaking, the war began in Malaya rather than at Pearl Harbor.

3. Platoon Leader

1. Bourke, *An Intimate History of Killing*, 67.

2. Wilbur Jones, *Gyrene: The World War II United States Marine* (Shippensburg, Pa.: White Mane Books, 1998).

3. On Iwo Jima, as an officer, Jim was issued the lighter-weight M1 carbine rather than the M1 Garand, which was the principal weapon of the enlisted men of a rifle platoon.

4. According to the Internet's Wikipedia site, the Rocket Launcher, M1A1, "was one of the first antitank weapons based on the HEAT shell to enter service, used by the United States Armed Forces in World War II. It was nicknamed 'bazooka' from a vague resemblance to the musical instrument of the same name." The bazooka "consisted of a four-foot tube with a simple wooden stock and sights, into which 60mm rocket grenades were inserted at the rear. A small battery provided a charge to ignite the rocket when the trigger was pulled. The main drawback to the weapon was the large backblast and smoke trail, which gave away the position of the shooter."

5. The Marine Corps organizational table was set up based on the principle that one man could effectively manage only three other men or units at a time. This principle applied from top to bottom. The Fifth Amphibious Corps (VAC) was composed of three divisions, the 3rd, 4th, and 5th. The 4th Marine Division was divided into three regiments, the 23rd, 24th, and the 25th. The designation when referring to the 24th regiment was "24th Marines." There was no 24th regiment in the other Marine Divisions (the Fifth Marine Division, for example, consisted of the 26th, 27th, and 28th Marines). A regiment was divided into battalions. There were three battalions in the 24th Marines — 1st, 2nd, and 3rd. Each battalion was further divided into three companies designated by a letter. In 1944 the 3rd battalion of any Marine regiment was divided into companies I, K, and L (there was no J company). Each company was divided into three platoons, 1st, 2nd, and 3rd. A Marine rifle platoon was the smallest unit designation. The hierarchy was thus, Division, Regiment, Battalion, Company, and Platoon. The usual complement of a rifle platoon in World War II was 45 Marines plus the platoon leader.

6. Some of these same boats had been used in the Normandy landings in France six months earlier. They were manufactured in New Orleans and named after their designer, Andrew Higgins.

7. D-Day was originally set for 20 January 1945.

4. Movement to the Objective

1. It was well known that memorizing the exact location of enemy positions on a beach targeted for amphibious assault usually did not make much difference in the final outcome. Landing parties rarely landed exactly where they were supposed to land, and bombing before the invasion often changed the landscape enough that it no longer resembled the pictures. Still, it was not a waste of time to review the maps and the pictures. It gave the Marines an idea of what the terrain was like and a general lay of the land. It also may have provided a psychological benefit to the men of knowing that they weren't going into the battle blind.

5. Welcome to Hell

1. Manchester, *American Caesar: Douglas MacArthur, 1880–1964*, 351.

2. News correspondent Keith Wheeler, who had witnessed the slaughter on Tarawa, said of the fighting on Iwo Jima, "There's more hell in there than I've seen in the rest of this war put together. The Nips have got the beaches blanketed with mortars. There are dead Marines scattered from one end to the other." Robert Sherrod, who had been with the Marines on Tarawa and Saipan, offered this chilling description to his readers of *Time* and *Life* magazines: "The first night on Iwo Jima can only be described as a nightmare in hell. About the beach in the morning lay the dead. They had died with the greatest possible violence. Nowhere in the Pacific have I seen such badly mangled bodies. Many were cut squarely in half. Legs and arms lay fifty feet from any body."

3. A gunwale is the upper edge of the side of a boat.

4. Ross, *Iwo Jima: Legacy of Valor*, 81.

5. Iwo Jima had an area of only about eight square miles. After the 3rd Marine Division landed, there were more than 70,000 Marines and more than 21,000 Japanese soldiers on the island, which meant that there were more than 11,000 combatants per square mile all trying to kill somebody.

6. Quote heard from the A&E History Channel video *Hell's Volcano*.

7. The stress of combat on Iwo Jima was simply too much for some of the Marines. Of the total casualties suffered during the battle 2,648 of them were due to "combat fatigue."

8. Bergerud, *Touched with Fire*, 381.

6. Into the Meat Grinder

1. The Marines used two types of satchel charges in the Pacific. One was a 20-lb. package with eight M3 or M4 C-2 plastic explosive blocks. The other was a 10-lb. M2 shaped-charge for blasting pillboxes.

2. For want of a nail, the shoe was lost.
　　For want of a shoe, the horse was lost.
　　For want of a horse, the rider was lost.
　　For want of a rider, the battle was lost.
　　For want of a battle, the kingdom was lost.
　　And all for want of a nail.
　　　　AUTHOR UNKNOWN

3. The versatile combat helmet had many uses for the enterprising Marine. At night in a foxhole, when it was not safe to venture out, it served as a toilet bowl.

4. Actually, according to Col. Joseph H. Alexander, USMC (Ret.), *Utmost Savagery—The Three Days of Tarawa*, this was an M89 50mm heavy grenade that the Marines mistakenly called a "knee mortar" because the curved monopod appeared to fit the gunner's knee. The M89's recoil would break bones if fired in this fashion.

5. Jim's brother, Syd, a B-29 bomber pilot, had to make an emergency landing on Iwo Jima before the war was over. In a very real sense, Jim and the Marines had made it possible for Syd to land on a runway rather than ditch in the ocean.

6. When the military leadership in Hawaii formulated its grand strategy for the defeat of Japan, it envisaged a shorter campaign than the four weeks it took to subdue the Japanese on Iwo Jima. The planned invasion of Okinawa, conceived months earlier, called for the 4th Division to be the reserve division, as the 3rd Division had been for Iwo Jima. But the 4th Division had been so badly mauled on Iwo Jima that these plans had to be changed.

Bibliography

Memoirs and Biographies

Arsenault, Maj. Albert. Unpublished memoir.

Bartley, Lt. Col. Whitman S. *Iwo Jima: Amphibious Epic.* 1954; reprint, Nashville: Battery Press, 1997.

Bergerud, Eric M. *Touched with Fire: The Land War in the South Pacific.* New York: Viking Press, 1996.

Berry, Henry. *Semper Fi, Mac: Living Memories of the U.S. Marines in World War II.* 1982; reprint, New York: Quill, 1996.

Bourke, Joanna. *An Intimate History of Killing: Face-to-Face Killing in Twentieth-Century Warfare.* New York: Basic Books, 1999.

Bradley, James, with Ron Powers. *Flags of Our Fathers.* New York: Bantam Books, 2000.

Brokaw, Tom. *The Greatest Generation.* New York: Random House, 1998.

Greene, Bob. *Duty: A Father, His Son, and the Man Who Won the War.* New York: William Morrow, 2000.

Jones, Capt. Wilbur D. *Gyrene: The World War II United States Marine.* Shippensburg, Pa.: White Mane Books, 1998.

Kerins, Jack. *The Last Banzai.* Privately published, 1992.

Kessler, Lynn, and Edmond B. Bart, eds. *Never in Doubt: Remembering Iwo Jima.* Annapolis, Md.: Naval Institute Press, 1999.

Manchester, William. *American Caesar: Douglas MacArthur, 1880–1964.* Boston: Little, Brown, 1978.

———. *Goodbye, Darkness: A Memoir of the Pacific.* Boston: Little, Brown, 1980.

Nalty, Bernard C., ed. *Pearl Harbor and the War in the Pacific.* London: Salamander Books, 2001.

Newcomb, Richard F. *Iwo Jima.* New York: Holt, Rinehart and Winston, 1965.

Prange, Gordon W. *December 7, 1941: The Day the Japanese Attacked Pearl Harbor.* New York: McGraw-Hill, 1988.

Proehl, Carl W., ed. *The Fourth Marine Division in World War II.* Nashville: Battery Press, 1989.

Ross, Bill D. *Iwo Jima: Legacy of Valor.* New York: Vanguard Press, 1985.

Russell, Michael. *Iwo Jima.* New York: Ballantine Books, 1974.

Tanaka, Yuki. *Hidden Horrors: Japanese War Crimes in World War II.* Boulder, Colo.: Westview Press, 1996.

Tatum, Charles W. *Iwo Jima: Red Blood, Black Sand.* Stockton, Calif.: privately published, 1995.

Toland, John. *The Rising Sun: The Decline and Fall of the Japanese Empire, 1936–1945.* New York: Random House, 1970.

Tregaskis, Richard. *Guadalcanal Diary.* New York: Random House, 1943.

Uris, Leon. *Battle Cry*. New York: Putnam, 1953.

Van der Vat, Dan. *The Pacific Campaign: World War II, the U.S.–Japanese Naval War, 1941–1945*. New York: Simon and Schuster, 1991.

Wright, Derrick. *The Battle for Iwo Jima*. London: Sutton, 1999.

———. *Iwo Jima 1945: The Marines Raise the Flag on Mount Suribachi*. Oxford: Osprey Military, 2001.

Young, Donald J. *First Twenty-four Hours of the War in the Pacific*. Shippensburg, Pa.: Bund Street Press, 1998.

Official Marine After-Action Reports

Final Report on Iwo Jima Operation, 3rd Battalion, 24th Marines, 4th Marine Division, Fleet Marine Force.

4th Marine Division Operations Report, Iwo Jima, February 19 to March 16, 1945.

Operational Report, 24th Regimental Combat Team.

JOHN C. SHIVELY has practiced occupational medicine since 1991, working in this capacity with Exxon in a corporate setting and in Terre Haute, Indiana, in a clinical setting. Shively has long had an interest in the history of World War II, but only recently has he begun to take an interest in writing about Hoosiers who fought in the Pacific War. He has traveled extensively in the Pacific to visit World War II battlefields.